Free Stuff
FOR
Gardeners
ON THE
INTERNET

Judy Heim and Gloria Hansen

C&T PUBLISHING

Copyright © 2000 Judy Heim and Gloria Hansen
Developmental Editor: Barbara Konzak Kuhn
Technical Editors: Steve Cook and Vera Tobin
Cover and Book Design: Christina Jarumay
Illustration on Front and Back Cover: Christina Jarumay
Book Production: Nancy Koerner

Library of Congress Cataloging-in-Publication Data

Heim, Judy.
    Free stuff for gardeners on the Internet /
    Judy Heim and Gloria Hansen.
       p. cm.
    Includes bibliographical references (p.174) and index.
    ISBN 1-57120-097-5 (paper)
    1. Gardening—Computer network resources—Directories. 2. Internet addresses—Directories. 3. Web sites—Directories. 4. Free material—Computer network resources—Directories. I. Hansen, Gloria. II. Title.
    SB450.955 .H45 2000
                           99-050855
                           CIP

Published by C&T Publishing
P.O. Box 1456
Lafayette, California 94549

Printed in China
10 9 8 7 6 5 4 3 2 1

DEDICATION

We dedicate this book to our husbands John and Rich, two of the most patient and meticulous gardeners we know. If gardening symbolizes marriage, both have blessed us with beautiful gardens, in our hearts as well as our homes.

We also want to thank the gardeners who share so generously of themselves and their wisdom on the Web. By sharing their knowledge and spirit they make the world a greener place, and hopefully a gentler, more beautiful one as well.

There are thousands of Web sites for gardeners. Sifting through them was a challenge. While we've tried to select sites that we think offer the most gardening advice, that doesn't mean there aren't many more out there that are equally illuminating and valuable. Also, because of the fluid nature of the Internet, it is inevitable that some of the Web sites in this book may have moved or even vanished. Had we included only those Web sites that are sure to be around many moons from now, this book wouldn't be nearly as valuable. While you can learn a great deal on the Internet, we encourage you to join a local gardening club or volunteer at a nature preserve or botanical garden. Learning about gardening on the Web is fun, but nothing can beat getting your hands dirty with your friends.

Judy & Gloria

Symbols in this book

 You can find lots of free goodies on the Web, but you'll learn more if you follow the chat icons and join in the many discussion groups offered on the Internet.

 This icon signifies a bit of Judy-and-Gloria hard-earned wisdom—in other words, something we wished we knew when we first started cruising the Web.

 When you see this icon, read carefully—and don't make one of the same silly mistakes we have!

 This icon means that the Web site also sells products that relate to the information on their site.

Table of Contents

CHAPTER 1

Why Gardeners Love the Web

Where do you turn when your hibiscus is drooping? Who do you talk to when strange brown spots speckle your otherwise green lawn? Who can you consult with when you and your spouse argue over how to prune the honeysuckle? Other gardeners on the Internet, of course! You can find an answer to literally any gardening question on the Web. There are thousands of Web pages devoted to gardening advice. Millions of gardeners tap into the Web nightly to share gardening wisdom in newsgroups and forums and correspond with other gardeners around the world about their gardens. No matter how obscure your plant passion, we guarantee that there are mailing lists and Web pages devoted to it. And this book will help you find them.

THIS BOOK WILL GET YOU ANSWERS TO YOUR GARDENING QUESTIONS—FAST!

A few years ago, you could tap just about any question into a Web searcher like Altavista (**http://www.altavista.com**) and find an answer with just a few mouse clicks. These days it's not so easy. The Web has exploded into the world's biggest library and shopping mall, with millions of Web sites and tens of thousands of discussion groups. Sorting through them to find what you need can be an arduous task. We've done the work for you. We've sifted through thousands of gardening Web sites and organized the best into chapters that will speed you to answers to your gardening questions. This book will lead you to:

• The biggest and best gardening Web sites, where you're most likely to find quick answers to your gardening problems.

• Web sites where you can download brochures from state extension services.

- Web sites with gardening advice specific to your climate.

- Discussion groups for gardeners. Correspond with other gardeners around the world about orchids, cacti, tropical hibiscus, or ponds. Whatever your gardening passion, there are other gardeners on the Web who share it and who are talking about it.

- Web sites that offer help culturing roses, pruning trees, growing perennials, raising vegetables, and attracting birds and other wildlife to your garden.

- Web sites that offer advice on landscaping. There are even Web sites where you can learn about "wild" landscaping—and which offer advice on keeping your neighbors happy.

AMERICA ONLINE IS A GOOD PLACE TO GET STARTED IF YOU'VE NEVER BEEN ONLINE BEFORE

AOL is a great way to get started on the Internet if you've never tapped into cyberspace before. But be warned, you may out-grow it fast. (A month after Judy and her husband got their parents on America Online, they were clamoring for faster access to the Web.)

You can get a free AOL startup disk by calling 800/827-6364, or have a friend download the software for you from America Online's Web site (**http://www.aol.com**). The software is also preloaded on many new systems, including the iMac (which Gloria's mom proudly owns).

Once you've installed the software and have connected to America Online, press **Ctrl-K** (or ⌘-K on a Mac), type the keyword **internet<enter>** or **web<enter>**, and you're on the Internet.

Among AOL's disadvantages are its hourly fees to access some areas of the service and the fact that the service's access numbers are long-distance calls for some. Also, AOL's numbers are sometimes busy in the evening (when all the kids are online). AOL also charges additional hourly access fees for anyone connecting from outside the continental United States or anyone calling through an AOL 800 number.

Tips for Tapping Into Gardening Advice on America Online

Use the keyword: **garden** or **gardening** to get to the gardening resources and forums on AOL. You'll find garden tips, a plant encyclopedia, a guide to public gardens, and gardening message boards.

Click the "Home and Garden Index" on the garden-ing main page to get a list of gardening resources avail-able on America Online. (By the way, stuff is hard to find on AOL. The main

searcher is crummy. Use the Home and Garden Index instead.)

Several home and gardening magazines host forums on America Online. To get to them, use the Home  and Garden Index. Or, use the keyword "**homemag**" to get to Home Magazine Online or "**wd**" to get to Women's Day Online.

There are over a hundred message boards on AOL devoted to gardening topics. To find them, use the keyword 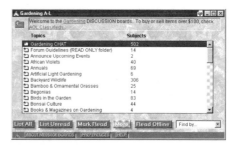 "**gardening**" and click on message boards on the main gardening screen.

To get to the Web from America Online type the Web page's address, or "URL," into AOL's keyword box—as in **www.bulb.com**  to the right. If you'd rather use Netscape instead of AOL's clunky browser, once you're connect to AOL, minimize the AOL software, then fire up Netscape and type the address of the Web page you seek.

Tips for Viewing Gardening Web Sites with AOL

Gardening Web sites are full of pictures. But sometimes the pictures may look smeary or may not appear at all. Here are tips for troubleshooting picture problems:

Clear Up Smeary Pictures—If you use Internet Explorer 5 to surf the Web with AOL, you may have noticed that IE 5 sometimes has problems displaying Web graphics. The culprit is AOL's graphics compression. Turn it off by heading to **My AOL/Preferences** and clicking the **WWW** icon. Head to the **Web Graphics** tab and remove the check beside "Use compressed graphics." Click **Apply.**

Clean Out Your Cache—Clean out AOL's cache directories and files regularly to keep the software from slowing down on the Web. Click **My AOL**, select **Preferences**, and click **WWW**. Under the General tab, click **Delete Files** under Temporary Internet Files, and under History, click the **Clear History** button. While you're there, click the **Settings** button under Temporary Internet Files and reduce the "amount of disk space to use" to store Web graphics to about 50 megabytes. A large cache file can slow down your Web sessions. Run Scandisk weekly.

Try a Different Browser—If you'd rather surf the Web with Microsoft's **Internet Explorer** or **Netscape**, once you connect to AOL, minimize the AOL software and fire up your favorite browser instead.

Power Down to AOL 3.0—If AOL's software seems to run slowly on your PC and if you have an older computer—a 486 or an older Pentium (or System 7.5 or under on a Mac), try installing an older version of AOL's software. You can download AOL 3.0 from AOL's Web site (**http://www.aol.com**).

IF YOU OUTGROW AOL AND DECIDE TO SHOP FOR AN INTERNET SERVICE . . .

Many people graduate from AOL to an Internet service provider (ISP) with local access numbers because of the better speed and reliability an ISP provides. Whether you sign up with a national ISP or a local one, shop for one with a fast connection of T1 or better, directly into the Internet's network backbone, and 56K bps connections that support the same connection standard as your modem does. Ask friends and neighbors for recommendations (you don't want an ISP that inflicts busy signals or is slow at delivering e-mail). Most ISPs offer unlimited Internet access for $20/month. That usually includes the ability to set up a Web site. Five megs is a good size to get you started.

Our picks for favorite national ISPs? AT&T's **WorldNet** (**http://www.att.net**) *and* Earthlink (**http://www.earthlink.com**).

Cable TV Offers High Speed Internet, but at a Price

Many local cable TV franchises offer Internet access through the same cable that sends you cable TV. With advertised connect rates of 10 megabytes per second, it's no wonder cable Internet is getting popular—although actual connect rates are considerably lower, depending upon what time of day you tap in. Cable Internet costs about $150 for installation, plus $40 to $50 per month. (That may be a good deal if you're getting gouged by local phone rates to call AOL or an ISP.) Cable Internet is presently available in limited areas of the country, though access is sure to grow. To find out if you can get it call your local cable TV franchise.

When you call for prices, ask how many outlets are included in the installation fee (cable TVs and cable modems can't connect to the same outlet) and make sure you can actually connect to the Internet before your cable installer leaves. You'll also need to find out if you get any space for a Web site; many cable companies don't offer the ability to set up a Web site.

Some people use a combination of America Online and cable access. If you decide to go this route sign up for AOL's "Bring Your Own Access" subscription option for the cheapest rate.

Satellite Is Pricey,
but the Only Option in Some Rural Areas

If phone calls to the nearest ISP are eating into your lifestyle and cable Internet isn't available in your area, consider accessing the Internet via satellite. The main requirements are a Windows 95 or NT-running PC, a direct line-of-sight to the southern horizon, and a lot of patience. Hughes Network System's DirecPC (**http://www.direcpc.com**) is the leading satellite Internet service.

 ## WHAT ABOUT "FREE E-MAIL" SERVICES?

There are two sorts of free e-mail services. There is **Juno** (**http://www.juno.com**), which gives you free software that you use to dial local access numbers and send and retrieve mail, and there are Web-based services like **Microsoft's Hotmail** (**http://www.hotmail.com**). You tap into these Web services through a computer that already has some Internet access—a work computer, for instance, or one at a library or cyber-cafe. Their advantage is that you can send and retrieve private e-mail through the service without using, for instance, your work e-mail address if you're tapping in through your work computer.

Juno is a great deal, especially if there's a local access number in your area. But all you get is e-mail, unless you pony up $20/month for Web access.

> ✋ **Warning!** There are some big disadvantages to using the "free e-mail" services like Juno and Hotmail. You may not be able to participate in some of the high-volume gardening discussion mailing lists. These lists generate lots of e-mail each day—so much mail that it will quickly fill up your mail box on these services and the mailing list owner will unsubscribe you in irritation. In fact, some mailing lists won't even permit people to subscribe who are using free e-mail services like Hotmail or Yahoo. It's best to get a "real" e-mail account with an ISP or online service like America Online.

◤ WHAT GARDENERS NEED TO KNOW
◣ ABOUT THEIR WEB BROWSER

Whether you tap into the Web through an Internet service or America Online, the software centerpiece of your Web surfing is what's called a browser. In the old days you needed different sorts of software to do different things on the Net. For instance, you needed mail software to send and receive e-mail; a news-reader to read public discussions; you needed special software called FTP (for "file download protocol") to download files to your computer. Plus, you needed a browser to view (or browse through) the graphical portion of the Internet known as the Web. Now all those functions are built into browsers.

Most computers are sold with Netscape's Navigator or Microsoft's Internet Explorer already installed. You can also download them for free from Netscape's Web site (**http://www.netscape.com**) or from Microsoft's (**http://www.microsoft.com**).

While you can use just about any computer to log onto the Internet in some fashion (even an original Apple II, circa 1979), to be able to view graphics you'll need a computer manufactured in at least the last 8 years. If you have an older computer, download a copy of the $35 **Opera** browser (**http://www.operasoftware.com**) which will run on any Windows 3.x-running PCs as old as 386SX's with 6 megabytes of RAM.

If you're running an older Macintosh, head to Chris Adams' **Web Browsers for Antique Macs** web page (**http://www.edprint.demon.co.uk/se/macweb.html**) to download Tradewave's MacWeb or an early version of NCSA Mosaic.

If you've never configured Internet software before, you'll need someone to help you, even if you're a computer genius (believe us, we know). Your ISP will (or should) give you direc-tions on how to set up Windows 95 or the Macintosh OS to at least log on to their service.

But once you're connected, you're pretty much on your own. That's why we've put together this little tutorial.

Note: The following directions are for the latest versions of Explorer and Navigator, but, with the exception of the instruc-tions for e-mail, most will work with earlier versions of the browsers.

HOW TO TAP INTO A WEB PAGE

To get to a Web page, such as that of **The Vegetable Patch**, a Web site for organic veggie growing, type its address (also known as its URL, or Universal Resource Locator) into the Address: bar in Navigator, or the Location: bar in Internet Explorer.

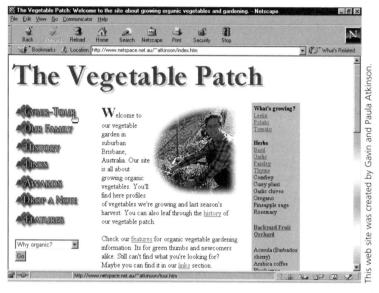

Take note that the case of the letters is important.

You can also cut and paste URLs from other documents into the address or location bar. Highlight the address with your mouse, press **Ctrl-C** (or ⌘-C on a Mac), then place the mouse in the location bar and press **Ctrl-V** (or ⌘-V on a Mac) to paste it in. Then hit **<Enter>**.

To move to other pages in the Web site, click on highlighted words, or, whenever your mouse cursor changes into a hand when its positioned on an object, right-click your mouse to go there.

How to Find the Web Site
if the Web Page Isn't There

URLs point you to directories on a remote computer just like directory paths (**c:\windows\programs**) get you to different directories and subdirectories on your computer's hard disk.

If a Web address doesn't get you to what you want, try working back through the URL. For example, Michigan State University offers a library of fact sheets on 1,800 vegetables and herbs at:

http://www.msue.msu.edu/msue/imp/mod03/master03.html

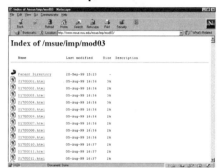

If it's not there when you get there, try:

http://www.msue.msu.edu/msue/imp/mod03

If there's nothing there, try: **http://www.msue.msu.edu/msue/imp**

And so forth. Should those URLs fail to display anything worthwhile, or if you get error messages, try Michigan State University's main page at
http://www.msue.msu.edu

What Does All that Gobbledygook in a URL Mean?

The **http:** tells your Internet service what kind of document you are trying to access on the Internet. HTTP stands for "hyper-text transfer protocol," the protocol of the Web. You might run into **ftp:**, which stands for "file transfer protocol," an early Internet scheme for transferring files. The protocol is always followed by "//" which separates it from the document's address.

Next comes the domain name. For example, **www.ctpub.com**. The triple-w designates C&T's Web subdirectory on its Internet server. The **.com** suffix indicates that C&T is a commercial entity. C&T would have an **.edu** suffix if it were a university, or an **.org** one if it were a non-profit. The words that follow the domain name, separated by slashes, designate further subdirectories. Many, though not all, URLs end with a specific file name.

Keep Your Browser Current to Keep Your Computer Secure

Hardly a month goes by without someone finding a new security hole in a popular browser—and its maker quickly plugging it. Keep your Web browser current—and your e-mail software too—by visiting the Web sites of their makers regularly and downloading any security patches or new versions. *Be sure you download those only from their makers' Web sites.* There have been reports of people receiving via e-mail "security patches" for Microsoft products that were actually hacker code to steal passwords. You can find out what version of Netscape you have by pulling down the Help menu and selecting About Communicator. If it's less than 4.5 you need to download a new version from Netscape's Web site (**http://www.netscape.com**). If you're running Internet Explorer, from the Help menu select About Internet Explorer. If you're running a version prior to 5.0, you need to download a new copy from Microsoft's Web site (**http://www.microsoft.com**).

FIND YOUR WAY AROUND THE WEB WITHOUT GETTING LOST

© Michael Longo, 1996, 1997, 1998, 1999

*Right-click on the **Back** button in your browser for a list of Web sites you've recently visited. Click on their names to return to them.*

- Click the **Back** button in your browser to return to previously visited Web sites.

- Click the **History** button or select the history feature from a drop-down menu to list previously visited URLs.

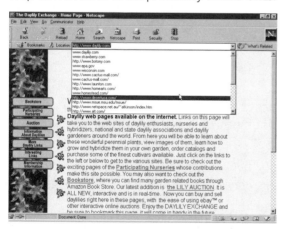

Click your browser's drop-down location box, which displays the last dozen or so URLs that you have actually typed into the browser (in other words, it doesn't display links that you've clicked on something to get to).

COMMON ERROR MESSAGES
WHEN YOU ENTER A WEB ADDRESS

✋ 404 Not Found

The requested URL /blocks/tips.html was not found on this server.

Reason: Your browser was able to find the Internet service or the computer on which the Web site was or is hosted, but no such page was found on the service. (The very last word "word" at the end of a URL is the page's address. For example, in this case it's **tips.html**.) Maybe the Web site owner removed that particular page. Or perhaps the Web site no longer exists.

Fix: Try working back through the URL as explained in the above tip, to see if you can locate the Web site, or determine if the site itself is gone from the service. Also, try suffixing the page's address with "htm" or "html" instead of its current extension. For example, in place of **tips.html** type **tips.htm**. (An HTML suffix is the same as an HTM, but some Web page hosting services require that Web pages be named with one or the other. Typing the wrong extension is a common mistake.)

✋ DNS Lookup Failure
or
Unable to locate the server.
The server does not have a DNS entry.

Reason: DNS stands for "domain name server." A domain name is the first part of a URL—for instance, in **www.ctpub.com**, **ctpub.com** is the domain name. Every Internet service (and AOL) has a database of such Web page host addresses. When you type a URL, the first thing your browser does is tell your Internet service to look up the domain name in its database, in order to find out where it's located. If it can't find it, your

Internet service's computer may poll other domain name directories around the Internet to determine if any of them know where the domain name can be found. If none of them do, you may get the error message "DNS Lookup Failure."

Why can't they find the domain name? Maybe it no longer exists. Or perhaps it's so new that the domain name databases your Internet service uses can't find it. Sometimes you also get this error message when there's heavy traffic on the Internet. Your Internet service is taking too long to look up the name, so your browser errors out.

Fix: Try typing the URL into your browser later in the day. If you still get the error message, try the URL a few days, or even a week, later. If you still get error messages, the domain name no longer exists.

No Response from Server

Reason: Your browser is unable to get a timely response from the Web site's host computer. This can be because of heavy traffic on the Internet, or on the branch of the Internet you are traveling. It can be because the computer that's hosting the Web site is overloaded (everyone is tapping in). Or it can be because your Internet service is overloaded, or its own computers are experiencing slowdowns for technical reasons.

Fix: Try the URL either in a few minutes, or later in the day.

Server Is Busy

Reason: A common error message issued by some heavily trafficked Web sites, this means that too many people are trying to tap in.

Fix: Try accessing the Web site later.

HOW TO USE BOOKMARKS

To add a bookmark to Explorer, click **Favorites/Add to Favorites**.
You can also drag URLs to the Link toolbar to create buttons.
Display the Links toolbar by heading to **View/Toolbars/Links**.

Web browsers let you "bookmark" sites so that you
can visit them again simply by fishing through your
bookmark catalog. You usually just click a bookmark
icon (or **Favorites** in Internet Explorer) or select the
feature from a toolbar to add to your bookmark list
the Web site that you're currently visiting.

***You Can Add Shortcuts to Web Sites on Your
Windows Desktop.*** Say there's a particular Web site
you like to visit everyday. If you're running Windows
95/98 you can add a shortcut to it from your desktop.
When you click on the shortcut your browser will load,
dial your Internet service, and speed you to the Web
site. Use your mouse to drag the site's URL from a link
in a Web page. Or, if you're using Internet Explorer,
drag from the Address bar to the left of the Links bar or
the Favorites menu. If you're using Netscape, drag the

icon to the left of Location: when a page is loaded. Your mouse cursor should change into a circle with a slash as you drag the URL to the desktop.

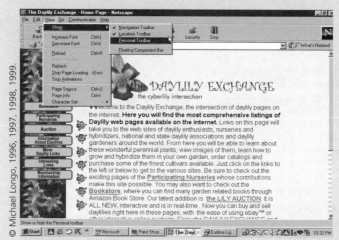

Create buttons on your personal toolbar in Netscape to whizz you to the Web sites you like to visit frequently. First, display the toolbar by pulling down the View menu, selecting Show, and placing a check beside Personal Toolbar.

Then, while the Web page is displayed, drag the Location icon to the Personal Toolbar just below.

While a Web page is displayed, right click on the page and select **Add Bookmark** from the pop-up menu.

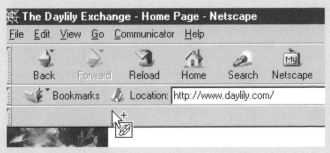

The icon should look like this while you're successfully dragging the Web site's location to your toolbar.

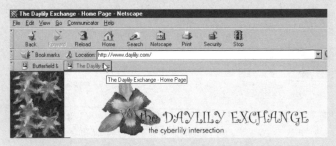

Click this button whenever you want your browser to take you to the Daylily Exchange Web site.

You Can Customize Your Browser's Personal Toolbar by Adding Bookmarks. You can customize the personal toolbar in Communicator or the Links bar in Internet Explorer by adding not only icons for frequently visited URLs but also folders of bookmarks. In Communicator add a URL to the personal toolbar by dragging a link from a Web page or by dragging the icon to the left of Location: when a page is loaded. To add a folder to the personal toolbar instead, click the Bookmarks icon, select Edit Bookmarks, and highlight the folder you wish to place on the toolbar. Right-click and select Set as Toolbar Folder. In Internet Explorer, you can similarly customize the Links bar by adding individual URLs as well as folders. Drag folders from the Favorites menu to add them to the Links bar. To add a URL to the Links bar, drag it from the Address bar to the left of the Links bar, from the Favorites menu, or from a Web page.

You Can Use Third-Party Bookmark Software to Organize Your Bookmarks. There are a lot of low-cost utilities for organizing bookmarks that you can download from the Web. These are particularly handy if you're using two browsers—both Netscape and Internet Explorer, for example. They enable you to store your bookmarks in a central location, and organize them into folders with icons—and in a more efficient manner than you can in your browser. Some utilities also let you password protect bookmarks. A good spot to download them is C/net's **Shareware.Com** (**http://www.shareware.com**). Search for the phrase "bookmark organizer." For PCs, one we like is the $29 shareware program LinkMan Professional from Thomas Reimann. For Macs, we like URL Manager Pro, the $25 shareware program from **Alco Blom** (**http://www.url-manager.com**).

 PRINTING WEB PAGES AND SAVING PICTURES TO DISK

To Print a Web Page

From your browser's menu select **Print**. If the page has frames you may need to first click on the frame that you want to print in order to select it. From the File menu, select **Page Setup** if you want to print the URL or date on the page (this feature is available only in newer browsers).

If you're using a Macintosh, we recommend the $10 shareware program Net-Print 8.1 from John Moe (**http://www93.pair.com/johnmoe**). It allows you to highlight any text and print or save it.

To Save a Picture to Disk

Position your cursor over the image and right-click. On a Mac, click-and-hold. A menu box will pop up. Select **Save Image As...** or **Save Picture As...** You can later view it in either your browser or a graphics program like Paint Shop Pro.

Judy & Gloria's Ten-Step Program for Fixing Browser and Graphics Crashes

After you spend an hour or so clicking around gardening Web sites your browser may start acting flaky. Maybe Web pages stop appearing so quickly or your computer grinds its disk a lot. Maybe your PC just locks up. Any number of things could be causing the problem. Follow these steps to make your life browser-crash-free:

STEP 1. Cold boot the PC. In other words, shut down your software, turn the power off, and turn it back on a few minutes later when the disk stops spinning. That will clean any flotsam out of its memory. Your browser will be flying again when you log back on the Web, but this solution is only temporary. Some people reboot their PC several times in the course of an evening. We think that's unnecessary. That's why we recommend the next steps.

STEP 2. Head to the Web sites of the maker of your PC, its video card, and its modem and download any fixes or new drivers.

STEP 3. Clean up your hard disk by running Scandisk and Disk Defragmenter. Click **Start/Programs/ Accessories/System Tools**. (You should do this every few weeks.) On a Mac, use Disktools available in the Extras folder on your OS CD.

STEP 4. If you're running Windows 95/98 head to Microsoft's Web site (**http://www.microsoft.com**) and download any new fixes, patches, or upgrades. (There are always fixes to download for Windows.) While you're there, download the current version of Internet Explorer and any fixes for that too, if that's the browser you run. If you use Netscape, get the newest one of that (**http://www.netscape.com**).

STEP 5. If you're running a version of AOL 3.0 earlier than 131.75, you need to upgrade. For AOL 4.0 upgrade if it's lower than 134.224. If you're running Windows 95 (or System 7.5 or earlier) and experiencing crashes with AOL 4.0 you might want to return to using AOL 3.0. Use the keyword "upgrade." To find out what version of AOL you're running, click Help/About America Online. Hit **Ctrl-R** when the AOL window pops up. To find out what version of AOL you're using on a Mac, launch AOL and select About AOL under the Apple menu.

STEP 6. A surfing browser will push your computer's memory to the limit. Try shutting down unnecessary applications while surfing and see if that helps. Press **Ctrl-Alt-Delete** to get a list of applications and close down everything but Explorer, Systray, and your browser. On a Mac, click the Finder Application Icon and Quit any unneeded programs. To troubleshoot your PC system further, right-click on My Computer and choose Properties. In the Device Manager tab, make sure that no red or yellow flags signal hardware conflicts. In the Performance tab, make sure that System Resources scores at least 85% free. Click the Virtual Memory button and select "Let Windows manage my virtual memory settings." Click OK. If AOL's crashing, you should try shutting down your virus software to see if that might be the source of the conflict.

STEP 7. Your browser needs lots of disk space for its cache. At least 50 megabytes or 10 percent of your disk should be free. You should empty your browser's cache weekly. Delete Netscape's history file (netscape.hst) and Cache folder. Clean out AOL's cache by heading to **My AOL/Preferences/WWW**. Head to the General tab and click the **Delete Files** and **Clear History** buttons. For Explorer, delete the folder Temporary Internet Files found in the Windows directory.

STEP 8. If Web page pictures look smeary or if your computer locks up while you're scrolling down a page, your video driver or graphics card may be at fault. Right-click on an empty spot in the desktop, click Properties. In the Settings tab change the Colors to 256. Click Apply. Under the Performance tab move down the Hardware Acceleration slider a notch. Click OK.

STEP 9. If your browser crashes while printing Web pages, it may be because your printer needs an updated driver. Or, it might need a bidirectional cable. Most printers are sold with bidirectional cables these days, but there's always that odd duck. But try this first: head to the Control Panel, click the Printer icon, and right-click on the icon for your printer. Select Properties. In the Details tab select Spool Settings. Set Print direct to printer. If there's an option to disable bidirectional support, do it.

STEP 10. If you think Netscape is at fault, head to Netscape's crash troubleshooting page (**http://help.netscape.com/kb/client/970203-1.html**). If you think Explorer is at fault, write down the Invalid Page Fault error message it spits out, then search for the message on Microsoft's tech support site (**http://www.microsoft.com/support**). Better yet, search for the names of your computer, your graphics card, and your modem on both Web sites. The chances are very good that you'll find your solution on one of them.

Here are more things to try:
• If you're feeling ambitious, download a new version of your browser, then uninstall your old one (this step is important). Then reinstall the new one.

- If Explorer spits out a Java or ActiveX error while trying to display a Web site, then goes belly up, try disabling these scripting languages. From the Tools menu, select Internet Options. Head to the Security tab and click the Internet icon. Click dots beside Disable in these categories: Download signed ActiveX controls; Run ActiveX controls and plugins; Active Scripting; and Scripting of Java applets. Under Java select Disable Java.

- If AOL is the source of your woes (the sign that the problem lays with your AOL software and not too many people logging on to the AOL network is that AOL freezes without the hourglass symbol), try deleting the AOL Adapter. From the Start menu select Settings, then Control Panel. Click the Network icon and head to the Configuration tab. Highlight "AOL Adapter" and click Remove. Restart Windows. Sign back on to AOL and AOL will reinstall an updated version of the adapter.

- Try calling a different AOL number and see if that remedies the freeze-ups. Head to My AOL/Access Numbers to find a new number.

- Use the keywords "Members Helping Members" to find up-to-date solutions to AOL freeze-ups.

Mac User Alert! If AOL crashes too many times in one week, a corrupt AOL Preferences file in the System Folder may be the culprit. To trash AOL's preferences file, first quit AOL. Then open the **System Folder/ Preferences/AOL/Preferences**. Drag only the AOL Preferences file to the trash. Upon relaunching, the program will create a new preferences file in the System File. This procedure also works for trashing a suspected corrupt Netscape preferences file.

Can't Find a Picture That You've Saved to Your Disk?

It happens all the time. You click on an image on the Web to save it to your computer, then you can't find it. If you can't remember the name of the graphic that you saved, go back to the Web page and click on it again to see the name. Then, if you have a PC running Windows 95/98, click Start, then Find and type the name of the file. Windows will find it for you. If you're using a Macintosh OS 8.5, go to the Apple menu and launch Sherlock. Click Find File and type in the name of the file. Sherlock will then find it.

If You Can't Access a Web Page Try These Tricks:

• If Netscape's logo keeps "snowing" but doesn't display any page, it may be because Netscape has frozen. Try accessing the Web site with Explorer instead. For convenience, cut the URL from Netscape's Location bar and paste it into Explorers.

• If you click on a highlighted link on a Web page but doesn't seem to get anywhere, try right-clicking on the link instead. From the pop-up box select "Open in New Window" or "Open Frame In New Window."

• If you click to a Web page with Netscape and the Web page appears to be blank, try accessing it with Explorer instead. Netscape is fussy about certain types of coding on pages and may refuse to load a page because it choked on some bit of coding.

• If a page doesn't appear to load properly, click the Reload button.

• If you're running Internet Explorer 5 and occasionally Web pages load only partially, you need to download a patch for Microsoft's Web site (**http://www.microsoft.com**).

⚡ HOW TO SEND E-MAIL

If you're using America Online, all you need to do is click on the You Have Mail icon on the greeting screen to read your e-mail or send mail, even out on the Internet. (To send messages to someone on the Internet from AOL, type the full Internet address—for example **info@ctpub.com**—into the **To:** line in the AOL mail screen, just as you'd type an AOL address.)

If you're using an Internet service, you can use special mail software like **Eudora** or **Pegasus**. Or, you can use the mail program built into your browser.

In Navigator, press **Ctrl-2** to get to Messenger, the mail program. On a Mac, click the **Mail** icon box in the lower-right hand corner of the browser's screen to get to your in-box. The command ⌘-T retrieves new e-mail.

In Explorer, click the **Mail** icon in your Windows 95/98 tray to load the Outlook Express mail program. On a Mac, click to **Mail** icon on your menu bar.

⚡ HOW TO READ USENET NEWSGROUPS WITH YOUR WEB BROWSER

Many talk groups for gardeners swirl through that raucous amalgam of newsgroups known as Usenet. But tapping into them can be tricky. You need to set up your browser to download the groups from your Internet service, then use your browser's mail reader to read them.

The first time you want to read a newsgroup you'll need to download a complete list of current newsgroups from your ISP. Then you'll need to search it and subscribe to the groups you're interested in. Finally, you need to download the messages themselves. Here's how to do it with Netscape and Explorer:

✋ *Warning to Parents!*

The Usenet newsgroups are unmoderated and uncensored. We spotted a lot of pornography in some of the newsgroups.

How to Read the Usenet Gardening Newsgroups with Netscape

1. You must first set up your browser to retrieve newsgroups from your Internet server. Find out from your Internet server the name of the computer where newsgroups are stored. (It will be something like **groups.myisp.com**.) Pull down the Edit menu and select Preferences. Under Mail & Newsgroups, head to the Newsgroup Servers or Group Server setup box, and click Add. Type the name of your ISP's newsgroup server. Click OK to save it.

2. Connect to your Internet service.

3. Head to Navigator's message center by pressing **Ctrl-2**, or click the **Mail** icon box in the lower-right hand corner of the browser's screen on a Mac.

4. From the **File** menu, select **Subscribe to Discussion Groups**.

5. Click the **All** or **All Groups** tab to download a list of current newsgroups. This may take a while since the list is large. The message "Receiving discussion groups" should appear on the very bottom line of the screen. Hit the **Refresh List** button if you, or someone else in your household has set up the newsreader to subscribe to mailing lists in the past.

6. When that humongous list of newsgroups has finished downloading, head to the Search for a Group tab. Type "**garden**" or "**agriculture**" (or whatever you're interested in) into the search box and click the **Search Now** button.

First you need to tell Navigator the name of the server on your ISP where newsgroups are stored.

You need to download the complete list of newsgroups in order to search for the ones about gardening.

7. Once the newsgroup searcher has come up with a list of interesting newsgroups, highlight the one you want to read, and press the **Subscribe** button. A check will appear beside it.

8. To read your newsgroup, head back to the message center (**Ctrl-2**, or click the **Mail** icon box on a Mac). From the pull-down menu box at the top of the screen, select the newsgroup and click **Download Messages**. Or, click the **Get Msg** icon. You may want to download only a selection (under 500, for example) and mark as read the rest of the messages. This way, the next time you download messages from the newsgroup, you will only download the newest ones.

9. From the **Go** menu you can move from thread to thread, reading messages and skipping others.

10. In the future to read messages, go to the message center (**Ctrl-2**, or click the **Mail** icon box on a Mac). From the pull-down menu box at the top of the screen, select the newsgroup you want to read. From the **File** menu, select **Get Messages/New**.

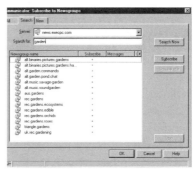

Search for the newsgroups about "gardening" or "agriculture" by heading to the search tab. After you've located the gardening newsgroups, subscribe to the ones you want to read by selecting them. You can click through the list just as you'd click through subdirectories on your computer.

Select the messages and message threads you want to read and they'll appear in the bottom of the screen. (If you don't get a split screen you may need to "pull up" the bottom portion of the screen with your mouse. In other words, the window is there, just hidden.)

How to Read the Usenet Gardening Newsgroups with Microsoft Explorer

1. Load the **Outlook Express** mail portion of Internet Explorer by clicking on the mailbox icon on the top right-hand corner of the screen. Click the **Read News** icon on the Express screen. If you have not yet set it up to read news-groups with your ISP, a setup wizard will appear. It will

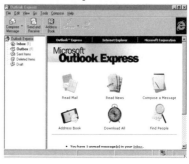

prompt you for your name, e-mail address, and the name of the dial-up connection you use to connect to your ISP. Most important of all, it will ask you the name of the server on your ISP where the news messages can be found.

2. The next time you click Express's **Read News** icon it will ask you if you'd like to download a list of the news-groups from your ISP. This may take a while, since there are tens of thousands of newsgroups.

3. Type "**garden**" to search the list for newsgroups that contain "garden" in their name. Subscribe to them by highlighting each, then clicking the **Subscribe** button. Then click **OK** when you're done.

4. To read newsgroups that you've subscribed to, click the **Go To** button. Or, click on the name of the newsgroup on the left side of the screen. To read individual messages, click on the headers displayed at the top right of the screen.

 Warning!

If you try to download more than about 500 newsgroup messages with Explorer, it will crash.

Read Gardening Newsgroups from Your Browser You can read newsgroups from the comfort of your Web browser by heading to **Dejanews** (**http://www.dejanews.com**). Reading them through this Web site isn't as easy as reading them with your browser's newsreader, but it's a simple way to access the groups.

KEEPING CHILDREN SAFE ON THE WEB

Be sure to supervise your children on the Net—the best way is to talk to them regularly about what they're doing online. Warn them as often as you can not to meet in person strangers they may meet online, even if they insist the new friend is a teenager—sometimes they're not.

Keep the kids away from the Usenet newsgroups where pornography is rife. If you're on AOL use the Parental Controls (keywords: **parental controls**) to block your child's access to Usenet. You should also block their screen name from receiving binary files (i.e. pictures) in e-mail.

How to Read the Usenet Gardening Newsgroups on America Online

1. To read the Internet newsgroups through AOL, press **Ctrl-K** (or ⌘**-K** on a Mac) and type the keyword: **newsgroups**. Click the Search All Newsgroups icon to search the tens of thousands of newsgroups for ones in your interests. (Some search words that work are: **garden**, **agriculture**, **forestry**, etc.)

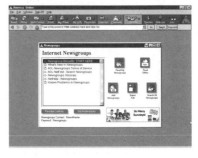

2. When AOL comes up with a list of matching newsgroups, click on the name of the newsgroup and from the pop-up box click "Subscribe to newsgroup." Depending upon which version of AOL's software you're using, you

can read the messages in the newly subscribed newsgroup immediately, or you'll need to head back to the main newsgroup menu by closing the windows (click the X in the upper right-hand corner). Click the **Read My Newsgroups** button to pop up a list of the newsgroups to which you're subscribed. Click the List Unread button to list messages in the newsgroups that you have not yet read.

3. To read listed messages click the title of the message. As you can see, there's a lot of junk floating around the forestry newsgroup on Usenet.

T I P

TIPS FOR STAYING SAFE ON THE WEB

The Internet is safer than the average subway station— but sometimes not by much. We know you're an adult and will take care of yourself just as you would in a subway station. But just so you know we're concerned about your safety, here are our motherly warnings:

• **Never give anyone your credit card**, any of your online passwords, or any personal information such as your street address or phone number. An all-too-common ruse is for hackers to e-mail a new subscriber to America Online alleging that they are a representative of AOL and need the subscriber to resubmit their credit card number for verification. Another ploy is for hackers to claim they work for Microsoft and to e-mail victims a "security patch" for Internet Explorer. Once the "security patch" is installed it e-mails the victims' passwords to the hackers. No one ever e-mails a security patch!

• **Don't open any file attachment that comes with an e-mail message from a stranger.** This is how viruses and Trojan horse programs (programs which snatch your passwords or do nasty things to your computer) are sent. Also, if you're on AOL, don't click on any hyper-link or Web addresses that arrives in your mailbox from a stranger.

• **Beware of get-rich-quick offers** that arrive by the megabyte in your e-mail box. And never answer junk e-mail. You might be bombarded with more e-mail, or the sender could retaliate if you ask to be removed from their mailing list. (That happened to a prominent woman in the craft industry. An angry junk e-mailer mail-bombed her company's e-mail server after she asked to be removed from his mailing list.)

• **If you shop on the Web, pay with a credit card** in case there are problems. Never type your credit card into any Web site that's not a "secure" Web site. That means that the site will encrypt the information you send it. As you enter a secure site your browser will tell you that it's secure. Also, Navigator will display a lock icon.

Having Problems with Your America Online Connection? Head to the Members Helping Members forum on America Online for the best tech support on the service. Type the keywords "**members helping members**" in the location bar at the top of the screen to get there. This will take you to a public discussion area where you're sure to find other members who are having the same problem as you are—or who know the solution.

When searching for Usenet gardening newsgroups some good keywords to search with include "**garden-ing**," "**agriculture**," "**forestry**," and "**environment**."

Big Web Sites with free Gardening Help

When our grandparents needed gardening advice they turned to their neighbors or that dour stack of *Progressive Farmer* magazines on the front porch. These days, if you ask your neighbor why your bonsai is looking peaked or your rhizomes spongy, they may well close the door on you. And have you ever returned to a chain store "gardening center" to ask why the dahlias you bought there look droopy? Fortunately, answers to your most puzzling gardening problems are as close as your computer keyboard. Tap into any of the Web sites in this chapter and it won't be long before the cacti on your windowsill are blooming and your gardening ambitions are spilling across acres.

Note: *Throughout this book we've noted with a "chat icon"* those gardening sites that offer chats, mailing lists, or message board discussion groups for gardeners.

SUITE 101—GARDENING
http://www.suite101.com/category.cfm/gardening

Tap into this portal to the world of gardening on the Web, where you'll find "guides" to over 50 gardening categories, from kids' gardening to beginning organic gardening. Each section on this portal site includes links to other Web resources, forums, and regular feature articles. Carol Wallace is the guide to this "cyber garden."

MS. GROW IT ALL
http://homearts.com/depts/garden/gro000c1.htm

Read columns by Sara Jane von Trapp, also known as Ms. Grow It All, the garden expert at Home Arts. She offers gardening how-tos in topics ranging from gardening basics to equipment, flowers, herbs, houseplants, landscaping, shrubs, trees, and vegetables.

THE VIRTUAL GARDEN
http://www.vg.com

Time-Life hosts this marvelous gardening site that offers help for novice gardeners as well as inspiration for those who were born with a green thumb. You can ask questions in the forums and tap into hundreds of how-tos that show you how to plant waterlilies, find your frost date in the fall, and raise leeks in the winter. The Plant Encyclopedia, compiled from Time-Life books, offers a searchable database of over 3,000 species of plants.

GARDEN.COM,
GARDENING FOR TODAY'S WORLD
http://www4.garden.com/index.html

Select the perfect plant for your garden with the plant finder, which includes a database of over 3,800 plants. Read news stories on what's hot in gardening, join chats, and read excerpts from Garden Escape magazine.

> **T I P**
>
> ### You Don't Need Acres to Grow a Garden
> Check out Window Box Gardening (**http://www.windowbox.com**) for tips and how-tos on growing flowers, veggies, and herbs in containers on your windowsill or porch.

GARDEN GUIDES
—A GROWING RESOURCE FOR GARDENERS
http://www.gardenguides.com

Dividing perennials, testing seeds for germinating ability, and help for container gardening are among the tutorials you'll find on this beautiful site. You'll also find a database of guide sheets to annuals, perennials, bulbs, herbs, and vegetables.

THE GARDEN WEB

The Garden Web sites provide links to gardening information around the Web, weather information, forums, and gardening contests, plus lots of gardening articles.

U.S. AND CANADIAN GARDEN WEB
http://www.gardenweb.com

U.K. GARDEN WEB
http://www.uk.gardenweb.com

AUSTRALIAN GARDEN WEB
http://www.au.gardenweb.com

GARDENNET
http://gardennet.com

Looking for someplace to buy carnivorous plants? Maybe you're hunting for a society of fellow camellia growers? GardenNet offers a large directory of suppliers and links to associations for different sorts of plants. You can also sign up for gardening mail-order catalogs and product information. If you'd like to visit well-known gardens while traveling, check out the garden guidebook, which lists hundreds of gardens around the world. If you're looking for gardening advice or want to share some, head over to the Gardener to Gardener Roundtable to discuss gardening questions.

🛒 BLOOM FROM HOME ARTS
http://www.homearts.com/depts/garden/00gardc1.htm

Want to know which vegetables can live for a hundred years or learn how to make a fresh herb wreath? Tap into this gorgeous Web site by magazine publisher Hearst. It includes links to garden tour information, seed swaps, and a gardener's library. A seasonal reminder feature will tell you what you need to do when depending upon the growing zone where you live.

Looking for a Gardening Club to Join?

Head to **Gardenscape's Gardening Societies and Organizations (http://www.gardenscape.com/GSOrgs.html)**, which offers a directory of gardening societies in the United States and abroad. The directory includes links to their Web sites.

If you're looking for a gardening club in the city where you live, check out **Garden Web's Garden Organizations Directory (http://www.gardenweb.com/directory/a-home.html)**. Clubs list volunteer needs and whether the club teaches classes or offers a master gardening program.

Or, head to **Cyber-Plantsman's Society Page (http://www.gardenweb.com/cyberplt/society)**.

Help for Gardening with Kids

Do you have little sprouts growing little sprouts? Head to the **Garden Center's Gardening With Kids (http://www.dlcwest.com/~createdforyou/sprouts.html)** for ideas for fun in the garden. The **4-H Children's Gardens at Michigan State University (http://commtechlab.msu.edu/sites/garden/contents.html)** features over fifty theme areas that you can explore in virtual reality.

Web site designed and produced by Matt MacQueen

WEB GARDEN
http://www.hcs.ohio-state.edu/webgarden.html

Ohio State University offers a wonderful collection of resources for both beginning and professional gardeners, including a plant dictionary, landscaping help, and special resources for Ohio and Midwestern gardeners.

HOUSE NET: LAWN AND GARDEN
http://www.housenet.com

Head to the Lawn and Garden section of House Net for lots of lawn and garden help. If you're new to gardening, you'll learn the basics of growing flowers, vegetables, and herbs. The service's creative gardening feature shows how to build window boxes and fashion topiary trees for the holidays. You'll also find regional tips, message boards, and a chat room.

🛒 INFODIGGER PRESENTED BY THE NATIONAL GARDENING ASSOCIATION & GARDEN SOLUTIONS
http://infodigger.gardensolutions.com/index.html

Type in a word like "bulb" and InfoDigger will search the National Gardening Association's database of more than 17,000 answered questions, 800 gardening tips, and 600 articles to find the information you need.

GARDENING AT ABOUT.COM
http://gardening.about.com

Deborah Simpson is your host for gardening on the Web with About.Com. Each week, she features new articles on topics ranging from making your own stones for your garden to growing plants that will attract butterflies. You'll find links to discussion groups and mailing lists for gardeners around the Web, plus links to other gardening Web sites and resources. If you have a gardening question, chances are you'll find a link to the answer here. There's also a free newsletter and gardening chats.

Looking for Even More Gardening Web Sites?
Head to **The Gardening Launchpad** (**http://www.tpoint.net/neighbor**) for links to over three thousand gardening Web sites.

Looking for Gardening Catalogs?

What gardener doesn't look forward to those January days when the spring gardening catalogs arrive in the mail? If you're itching to get on the lists of more mail-order catalogs, head to **Mail Order Garden Catalogs** (**http://www.mertus.org/gardening/cat17/frame-cat.html**). Cyndi Johnston has compiled a directory of over 1,751 catalogs, divided into topics like bulbs and roses. Then head to Joe Robinson's **Plants By Mail FAQ** (**http://pbmfaq.dvol.com/index.html**). It is intended to "introduce readers to the world of buying plants by mail order; and also to serve as a central clearinghouse for information about contacting various mail-order plant houses." You can find more lists of catalogs at I Can Garden (**http://icanGarden.com/gardcat.htm**) and **Gardenscape's Gardening Companies** (**http://www.gardenscape.com/GSCompaniesWWW.html**).

I CAN GARDEN
http://icanGarden.com

This Canadian gardening Web site offers feature articles, Canadian weather help, a kids gardening corner, special features on house-plants, and much more. Links to gardening catalog Web sites will get you the catalogs you need, and you'll also find links to gardening club Web sites.

BETTER HOMES & GARDENS GARDENING GUIDE
http://www.bhglive.com/gardening

Read weekly garden features, lots of garden planning advice, and answers to gardening questions, plus tap into a guide to garden projects.

Free Desktop Garden Pictures

Decorate your computer screen with free garden pictures from **Purdue University** (**http://www.hort.purdue.edu/hort/ext/HortGardenPictures**). You'll find downloading and installing instructions for both PCs and Macs on the Web site.

Download Free Demos of Gardening Software

Like to use your computer to help plan your garden or keep track of your seed stock? There are many programs you can download from the Web that will help you. The first place to check is **Cornucopia!'s Shareware Library** (**http://www.mnsinc.com/cornucopia/software.htm**). Cornucopia! offers links to numerous gardening programs including Gardener's Assistant, Horticultural Manager, Organize! Your Plants & Garden, Window Garden, and The Seed Program. You can also download demos or trial versions of gardening programs from the following Web sites.

Shareware is software that you try before you buy. You download either a full-featured or limited version from the maker's Web site or a shareware library. If you like it, you mail its author the registration fee. Freeware, on the other hand, is software that's distributed for free.

Note: Head to Chapter 18, Free Help for Landscaping and Garden Design for more software recommendations.

ABRACADATA'S SPROUT GRAPHIC VEGETABLE GARDENING DESIGN
http://www.abracadata.com/sp.html
Plan your garden and schedule your planting with this software for DOS, Windows, and Mac users.

MAKEITGROW BY JOHN SPICER
http://www.alberts.com/authorpages/00013285/prod_135.htm
A garden layout program for the Mac.

PLANTS FOR WINDOWS BY CHRIS RUNDLE
http://www.source.co.uk/users/cpr/P4W.HTM
Maintain a plant database, and print catalogs and labels with this Windows software.

ED HUME SEEDS' SOFTWARE
http://www.humeseeds.com/software.htm

Moonbook is a Windows calendar to organize your gardening by the signs of the moon and times of the year, and Successful Seed Gardening will help you grow plants from seed.

T I P

Looking for Botanical Gardens to Visit While Traveling? Head to Gardenscape's Arboreta, Botanical Gardens, Gardens, Herbariums Page (**http://www.gardenscape.com/GSGardens.html**). You'll find gardens in both the United States and abroad. Bontanique's Tour Garden and Arboreta Navigation Page (**http://www.botanique.com/tourmast.html**) lists tour gardens in the United States and Canada.

Funky Gardening Web Sites We Just Love

The following Web sites are fun, funky, and tell you about plants (and planting practices) that you may have never dreamed possible.

 GOTHIC GARDENING
http://www.gothic.net/~malice
Something wicked this way grows. This site features gothic gardens, gothic plant tales, and other plants that go bump in the night.

NORTH WEST FUNGUS GROUP
http://ourworld.compuserve.com/homepages/pfh2/nwfg.htm
Paul F. Hamlyn tells you everything you want to know about fungus.

GARDENING IN THE CABBAGE PATCH, FAIRBANKS, ALASKA
http://www.ptialaska.net/~pbabcock/patch
Pat Babcock shares a collection of gardening articles she wrote for the Fairbanks Daily News Miner *in the early '80s.*

COLD HARDY TREE FERNS
http://www.angelfire.com/wa/margate/treefernspage.html #introduction
Learn about growing ferns that can double as trees.

SCOTT'S BOTANICAL LINKS
http://www.ou.edu/cas/botany-micro/bot-linx
Dr. Scott Russell, of the University of Oklahoma's Department of Biology and Microbiology, maintains a fascinating collection of plant-related articles and Web links. For example, read about how trees planted 30 years ago in Ohio were evaluated for their suitability as urban street trees. Read about prairie building resources on the Web—and even prairie building games. This is a great site to visit every week to see what's new.

free Web Sites of TV Shows for Gardeners—and Free Gardening Radio Shows You Can Listen to On the Web

Most gardening TV shows host Web sites where you can tap into show schedules and sometimes even read tutorials and articles that elaborate on show segments. The best show Web site is for *Rebecca's Garden*. You'll find recipes, how-tos, message boards, and project ideas. There's even an online garden planner that will help you determine your growing zone and select plants.

There are many other gardening-show Web sites that offer special features and resources for gardeners. If you're a regular viewer of a show, bookmark its Web site and visit it regularly.

As of yet, there are no gardening TV shows that are broadcast on the Web. But you can listen on the Net to lots of gardening radio programs, many of them live. The second half of this chapter tells you how to find them and how to set up your browser to listen.

Web Sites of TV Shows for Gardeners

PBS GARDENING SHOWS
http://www.pbs.org
Head to the main PBS Web site and use the search feature to search for these shows, or search for the word "gardening."

• The Perennial Gardener with Karen Strohbeen
Transform your computer desktop into a perennial garden with a free download, get plant and flower lists from show episodes, and read Karen's gardening tips.

• The Victory Garden
You can tap into a show schedule of this popular PBS show.

• Nature: The Secret Garden
Kids will enjoy the features on the PBS Web site that were created to accompany the "Secret Garden" episode of Nature.

REBECCA'S GARDEN
http://www.rebeccasgarden.com

The Web site for Rebecca's Garden *TV show and magazine offers a how-to section with crafty tutorials on creating rose potpourri and floral centerpieces, plus how-tos on topics like growing vegetables in the fall. The site also offers links and information on garden tours around the country.*

Tap into the Web site of Rebecca's Garden
(http://www.rebeccasgarden.com*) for how-tos and gardening tips that elaborate on show segments.*

MARTHA STEWART LIVING
http://www.marthastewart.com/channels/garden.asp

THE WISCONSIN GARDENER
http://www.wpt.org/garden/index.html
Tap into the Web site of this Wisconsin Public Television show for resources and tips geared for Midwest gardeners.

CBC TV CANADIAN GARDENER
http://tv.cbc.ca/canadiangardener

Tap into the Web site of Canadian Gardener *for show schedules, contests, and links to other Canadian gardening resources on the Web.*

BETTER HOMES AND GARDENS TV
http://bhglive.com/tv

Read through the highlights of recent shows, download featured recipes, search the archives for gardening tips and more. There's a handy map to help you find local stations and air times.

HOME & GARDEN TV GARDENING SHOWS
http://www.hgtv.com

HGTV is home to many popular gardening shows. Tap into the main HGTV Web site to access features and schedules of the shows. The HGTV Web site frequently changes, so we're reluctant to list specific possibly short-lived URLs. Head to the site's searcher to search for features and schedules of your favorite gardening shows.

Way to Grow	**Landscape Smart**
Breaking Ground	**Gardening by the Yard**
The Great Outdoors	**CityScapes**
Gardener's Journal	**A Gardener's Diary**
The Winter Gardener	**World Garden Tour**
Rebecca's Garden	**Grow It Gardeners Guide**
Surprise Gardener	**Landscape Smart**
Garden Architecture	

Listen to Gardening Radio Shows from Around the World—Live on the Web!

Would you like to listen to Jerry Baker's gardening radio show, but despair that it's not broadcast in your community? Listen to it on the Web. A growing number of Web-cast mega-sites like Broadcast.Com (**http://www.broadcast.com**) broadcast radio shows—and some TV shows too. Some shows are broadcast live. But some you can listen to at any time of the day.

Here's how it works: You install one of the free browser plug-ins that plays audio and video—RealPlayer from RealNetworks or Windows Media Player from Microsoft. (We like to have both on hand.) You tap into a broadcasting Web site like Broadcast.Com. You click on the broadcast link for the show you wish to see and—voila!—the show pops up on your screen or plays through your computer's speaker.

Look for this logo to the free broswer extension for RealPlayer.

To listen to your favorite gardening radio show through Broadcast.Com, install the free Web browser plug-in RealAudio, then simply click on the show's link on Broadcast.Com's page.

http://www.broadcast.com/personalinterests/lawngarden

*Broadcast.Com (**http://www.broadcast.com**) offers live Web broadcasts of dozens of radio shows for gardeners.*

What You Need:

• A 486 DX or faster PC (Macintosh users need a Power PC 604 or better and System 8.1 or higher).

• A sound card and speakers.

• A reasonably good 28.8K or faster connection to the Net. (Needless to say, a faster connection is better.)

• An up-to-date Web browser. Head to the Web site of **Netscape** (**http://www.netscape.com**) or **Microsoft** (**http://www.microsoft.com**) and download the newest version of the one you use. You'll need a browser that supports Java and JavaScript. Versions of Internet Explorer prior to 5 are unable to play RealAudio files through certain dynamic links like an **.asp** script.

• The free browser plug-in RealPlayer from **RealNetworks** (**http://www.real.com**) or Windows Media Player from **Microsoft** (**http://www.microsoft.com**). We like having both on our computers. Both work with both Netscape and Internet Explorer browsers.

Tips for Getting Good Sound and Pictures

• Whether you use RealPlayer or Windows Media Player, keep your multimedia plug-in current by downloading new versions from the makers' Web sites as needed. This will help ensure good sound and video.

• Keep your computer's audio and video drivers current by occasionally visiting the Web site of your PC's maker and checking for any driver updates. Out-of-date audio drivers sometimes choke on compressed audio streams from broadcast Web sites.

• Clean out your browser's disk and memory caches regularly to keep audio and video error messages at bay. For instance, if your multimedia player displays an "error 14," it's usually due to a loaded cache. You might also want to increase the size of caches to handle large media files; you'll need to experiment with this. In Netscape head to **Edit/Preferences** and click **Advanced** to expand it. Select **Cache**. In the menu on the right side of the screen, click **Clear Memory Cache** and **Clear Disk Cache**. Click **OK**, then close and reload your browser. In Explorer, from the Tools menu, select **Internet Options** and head to the **General** tab. Under **Temporary Internet Files**, click the **Delete Files** button, then **OK**. Close and reload your browser.

• If you get "network congestion" errors, that means that a lot of other people are on the Net—or your ISP is overloaded. You may need to try watching (or listening) later in the evening, when there isn't as much traffic on the Web.

• If you get timeout errors, it may be because the broadcast server is overloaded from other users. It may also be because your ISP has heavy traffic.

• If you can't connect to the broadcast server at all, it may be because many other people are trying to tap in. These broadcast sites can only handle a limited number of viewers at once.

• When you're using RealPlayer, tweak the sound to work more efficiently with your sound card by pulling down the View menu and selecting Preferences. Under Sound Card Compatibility click the Settings button. Try selecting either Disable 16-bit sound or Disable custom sampling rate, then click OK. If the music doesn't sound any better try disabling the other setting. Check the Bandwidth setting found in the Connection tab to make sure it's set to the speed of your modem.

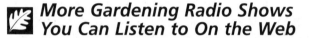 Where to Find Web Broadcasts of TV & Radio Shows

BROADCAST.COM
http://www.broadcast.com
Click on "Shows" to get a sampling of lawn and garden related broadcasts, or use the search function to find just the thing you want to watch.

GARDENING SHOWS ON BROADCAST.COM
http://www.broadcast.com/personalinterests/lawngarden

More Gardening Radio Shows You Can Listen to On the Web

TALKING PLANTS
The Talking Plants Web site is a new radio show on National Public Radio. You can hear excerpts at
http://www.talkingplants.com/radio.

THE DIRT DOCTOR
Listen to Howard Garett on his Web site at
http://www.dirtdoctor.com.

PERRY'S PERENNIAL BROADCASTS
Listen to the broadcasts of Dr. Leonard Perry, perennial maven at the University of Vermont, at his Web site:
http://moose.uvm.edu/~pass/perry.

free Stuff from Web Sites of Garden Magazines

Many gardening magazines host beautiful Web sites. They publish features from the print version of the magazine, breathtaking photos, and even special features written especially for the Web. Some include archives of past articles, which you can search for topics that interest you. Many host gardening message boards. Magazine Web sites are great sites to bookmark and visit regularly.

There are hundreds of gardening magazine Web sites. We've included our favorites in this chapter. For more gardening magazine Web sites, check out Deborah Simpson's Web magazine guide at **About.Com's Gardening (http://gardening.about.com)** and **Gardenscape's (http://www.gardenscape.com/GSMagsBooks.html)** magazine list.

You'll Find Electronic Gardening Magazines on the Web Too

We also included a guide to "e-zines"—electronic magazines or newsletters—for gardeners. These are free magazines or newsletters that you can read by tapping into a Web site each month or by signing up for an e-mail list. In the case of the latter, the "e-zine" will be mailed to your e-mail box each month.

Our Favorite Web Sites of Gardening Magazines

NATIONAL GARDENING ASSOCIATION'S NATIONAL GARDENING
http://www.garden.org
http://www.garden.org/edit/search.asp
http://www2.garden.org/nga/EDIT/home.html
The NGA's article archive is a wonderful resource for gardeners! Search it by subject to read articles full of inspiration and advice on solving your gardening problems.

REBECCA'S GARDEN
http://www.rebeccasgarden.com

At the cyberhome of Rebecca's Garden magazine and TV show, you can sign up for a free gardening tips newsletter, download recipes and flower craft instructions, and read special features.

MARTHA STEWART LIVING
http://www.marthastewart.com
Tap into Martha's Web site for information on the gardening segments of her TV show as well as articles related to the magazine.

COUNTRY LIVING GARDENER
http://homearts.com/clg/toc/00cghpc1.htm
Read features from the magazine and view a gallery of gardens.

BETTER HOMES & GARDENS
http://www.betterhomesandgardens.com
You'll find many features about gardening, projects, and a library of weekly gardening features.

GARDEN GATE
http://www.augusthome.com/gardeng.htm

You can look up advice on a variety of gardening topics. There are many detailed how-tos on topics like "irrigation made easy" and how to deer-proof your garden.

FINE GARDENING
http://www.taunton.com/fg/index.htm
Read weekly features and how-tos for projects like building a classic planter box and a bird-safe slug catcher from this Taunton Press publication.

KITCHEN GARDENER
http://www.taunton.com/kg/index.htm
Plenty of articles and tips such as how to grow a hundred pounds of potatoes in a three-foot space.

GARDEN ESCAPE
http://www4.garden.com/index.html
Read articles from the magazine, plus special features for the Web, at Garden.Com.

ORGANIC GARDENING
http://www.organicgardening.com
Read articles on attracting wildlife to your garden and more from this Rodale publication.

THE WEEDPATCH GAZETTE: FINE PLANT & GARDEN QUARTERLY FOR THE UPPER MIDWEST
http://www.weedpatch.com
Great articles and hot news from this esteemed publication for agricultural Zone 5. There's also an online plant catalog.

EAST COAST GARDENER
http://www.klis.com/fundy/ecg/home.htm
A magazine written for Atlantic Canada gardening zones, this site features a selection of articles from current issues.

TRADITIONAL GARDENING: A JOURNAL OF PRACTICAL INFORMATION ON CREATING & RESTORING CLASSIC GARDENS
http://traditionalgardening.com

Articles from the current issue, archived articles, garden sources and more.

COASTAL GROWER
http://www.coastalgrower.com

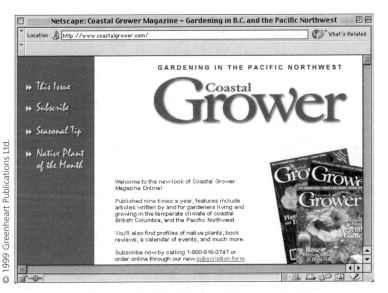

Includes tips and plant of the month. This publication, printed nine times a year, is geared for the temperate climate of coastal British Columbia and the Pacific Northwest.

PLANTS
http://www.plants-magazine.com
Many articles to read from back issues of this UK gardening magazine. You can also sign up for a free newsletter.

CONSUMER HOME & GARDEN MAGAZINE
http://www.consumer.org.nz/home/index.html
The Web site of this New Zealand magazine offers articles from the current issue. You can also obtain a free copy of previous issues.

BBC'S GARDENING WORLD
http://www.gardenersworld.beeb.com/index.shtml
Plenty of gardening articles, tips, projects, and more, from Britain's best-selling gardening magazine.

CANADIAN GARDENING
http://www.ab.sympatico.ca/mags/cangardening

GARDENS WEST
http://www.gardenswest.com/index.html
An archive of articles from past issues at the Web site of this magazine for Western Canadian gardeners.

 # Free Electronic Gardening Magazines or "E-zines"

  VIRTUAL GARDENER
http://www.beseen.net/virtualgardener/magazine.htm

Clyde Snobelen is the publisher of this online magazine with "organic roots." Its lively message board has three topic areas—insects, pests, and diseases; general gardening; and lawns and turf grass. Feature articles include how to attract hummingbirds and butterflies, and landscape design.

GLOBAL GARDENER
http://www.global-garden.com.au
Australia's first national monthly online gardening magazine.

THE CYBER PLANTSMAN
http://gardenweb.com/cyberplt
An online publication from The Garden Web.

 ### GARDEN LIFE
http://www.pressdemo.com/garden/garden.html
The Press Democrat of Santa Rosa, California publishes gardening features and hosts a question and answer forum on topics like vegetables, organics, flowers, resources, and more.

 ### GARDEN HELP
http://www.gramarye.u-net.com
A free Internet gardening magazine.

GARDENER'S EDGE
http://www.gdninfo.com/home5.html
Features a monthly plant, monthly almanac, and gardening advice.

TROPICAL GARDENING
http://www.tropicalgardening.com
Includes advice on planning a tropical landscape, among other topics. Archives of back issues available.

 **Visit The Free E-mail Newsletter Guide at About.Com's Gardening Forum** (**http://gardening.about.com/library/weekly/aa081898.htm**) for a directory of gardening newsletters you can sign up for.

DIG
http://www.digmagazine.com

This site features technique articles and topics including design, maintenance, perennials, plants, techniques, and more.

Dig Magazine *hosts a marvelous Web site where you can chat with other gardeners and read lots of wonderful features.*

Looking for Gardening Magazines?
If you're looking for magazines to subscribe to, check out **Barnes & Nobles'** magazine database and subscription service (**http://www.barnesandnoble.com**). They have (we think) one of the nicest magazine selections on the Net, and also the easiest to search for publications in your interests.

THE WEEKEND GARDENER
http://www.chestnut-sw.com

An electronic gardening guide with practical horticulture information geared for busy people.

 Discussion Groups for Gardeners

Our grandparents shared gardening tips over the backyard fence. These days, many share their gardening wisdom through AOL forums and Internet chat rooms. Corresponding with other gardeners around the world is great fun. It's also a great way to find gardening inspiration and get answers to your gardening problems. Who else but another gardener on the Web would encourage you to take the plunge and buy those miniature African violets you've always wanted but feared would perish under your brown thumb? And who else but another gardener would encourage you to ignore the protestations of your spouse and plow under the front yard to plant a Japanese meditation garden? Whether your gardening ambitions are confined to a few herb plants outside the kitchen door or sprawl across acres as wide as your dreams, you owe it to yourself to join some of these gardening discussion groups.

You'll find gardeners corresponding in:

• **E-mail or mailing list discussion groups**. To join you send an e-mail message to a computer. Messages from other group members are deposited in your e-mail box each day.

• **Bulletin boards.** You tap into a Web site and read messages that other gardeners write on different topics. You can respond to the messages either publicly or privately.

• **Newsgroups.** Newsgroups are public discussion groups whose messages swirl through cyberspace in a sort of bulletin-board-type free-for-all. To participate in newsgroup discussions; you need to set up your Web browser or AOL's software to "subscribe" you to the newsgroup, then download any new messages whenever you log on to the Internet. See Chapter 1 for directions on setting up your Web browser to join.

The Best Gardening Advice Is in Mailing Lists

Your best source of gardening information on the Net is likely to come from other gardeners in e-mail discussion groups.

You'll find special interest mailing lists in topics ranging from greenhouses to gourds, drip irrigation to daffodils, hot peppers to heirloom gardening, orchids to growing flowers on the Canary Islands.

There are literally hundreds of e-mail mailing lists for gardeners. To find ones in your interests we suggest checking out the following directories:

MAILING LISTS FOR GARDENERS BY KAREN FLETCHER
http://www.prairienet.org/garden-gate/maillist.htm

GARDENSCAPE
http://www.gardenscape.com/GSMagsBooks.html

GLOBAL GARDEN
http://globalgarden.com

You should also search the mailing list director Liszt (**http://www.liszt.com**), which maintains a directory of gardening mailing lists.

Other Places You Can Find Gardeners Chatting It Up

You'll find many avid gardening communities and mailing lists at these sites. You can also start your own gardening mailing list through these sites—for free!

DEJANEWS COMMUNITIES
http://www.deja.com
Head to "communities" and search the communities page for "gardening" or your specific gardening passion.

ONELIST
http://www.onelist.com
Use Onelist's search box to search for "gardening" or other gardening-related words.

Warning!
Do not sign up for mailing lists with "free e-mail" services like **Juno**, **Hotmail**, or **Yahoo Mail**. These lists generate lots of e-mail each day—so much mail that it will quickly fill up your mail box on these services and the mailing list will unsubscribe you. In fact, some mailing lists won't even permit people to subscribe who are using free e-mail services.

Gardening Mailing Lists Are Fun and Informative, but You Need to Follow the Rules

No matter what your interests, mailing lists are your best source of information on the Internet. But before you sign up for one, you should read its rules for joining and posting to the list. Then, follow our tips on mailing list netiquette.

• **When you join a mailing list, the computer that runs the list will automatically mail you directions for participating. Print them, and keep them near at hand.** Take note of the list's different e-mail addresses. You will be sending mail to one address, and sending any subscription changes to a different "administrative" address. *Don't send messages to subscribe or unsubscribe to the list to the main address, it will broadcast your message to everyone on the list!*

• **You probably have only a limited amount of disk space on your ISP to store incoming e-mail. That means that if you're a member of a mailing list that generates lots of mail, the mail may overrun your mailbox if you don't check your e-mail daily.** When that happens, e-mail that people send you will bounce back to them. And the list may automatically unsubscribe you because messages are bouncing back. The solution is to subscribe to the digest version of the list, if one is available, and unsubscribe from the list if you're going out of town.

• **If the mailing list has rules about how mail to the list should be addressed, follow them.** Many lists request that members include the list's name in the Subject: line of any messages so that members who have set up their e-mail software to filter messages can do so effectively. You should also try to make the Subject: line of your message as informative as possible for readers who don't have time to read every message posted to the list.

• **Never include your address, phone number, or other personal information in a mailing list post.** Many mailing lists are archived—which means that everyone on the Internet might be able to read them until the end of time!

• **Take a look at the message's address to check where it's going, before you hit the Send button.** Don't send a personal reply to everyone on the mailing list. And don't hit Reply to All if the message is addressed to many different people or lists.

Here are a few mailing list terms you might encounter:

Moderated List—All messages that are mailed to the list are first sent to a moderator to screen before being broadcast to everyone on the list. No, it's not censorship, but merely a tactic to keep messages to the topic under discussion, and, on some lists, to prevent "flame wars" from breaking out between disagreeing members.

Unmoderated List—Messages are not screened.

Digest—Messages are collected into one long e-mail message that is sent at the end of the day to members who subscribe to the list's "digest version."

Archive—Some mailing list messages are stored in vast libraries on a Web site for others to search and read years later.

FAQ—Most lists have a "frequently asked question" file that contains questions to answers that list members commonly ask. Usually the FAQ is stored on the list's Web site, although some lists allow members to retrieve the file through e-mail.

Free Gardening Bulletin Boards

There are as many Web sites that offer message boards for gardeners as there are weeds in Judy's lawn. Many of the big gardening Web sites we recommend in Chapter 2 host message board communities. Here are a few of our favorites:

THE GARDEN WEB'S FORUMS
http://www.gardenweb.com/forums

THE GARDEN WEB'S EUROPEAN FORUMS (MULTILINGUAL)
http://www.uk.gardenweb.com/forums

THE GARDEN WEB'S AUSTRALIA FORUMS
http://www.au.gardenweb.com/forums

SUITE 101—GARDENING
http://www.suite101.com/category.cfm/gardening

HEARST'S HOME ARTS FORUM OF GARDENING
http://homearts.com/discussion/ha/main/gacnvpot.htm

SIERRA HOME GARDENING MESSAGE BOARD
http://forums.sierra.com/forums/gardening

REBECCA'S GARDEN FORUM
http://forum.rebeccasgarden.com

GARDEN CENTER—FORUM
http://www.familygardening.com/forum.html

GARDEN TOWN—GARDENING FORUM
http://www.gardentown.com/chat/chat.html

DELPHI'S GARDEN GUIDES FORUM
http://www.delphi.com/gardenguides/start

HOME & GARDEN CONFERENCE
http://www.freenet.msp.mn.us/conf/home_and_garden

MINIATURE ROCK GARDENS FORUM
http://www.onelist.com/subscribe/miniaturerockgardens

Gardening Web Rings

A Web ring is a linked group of kindred Web sites organized around a particular theme, such as rose growing. You can visit sites in the ring by clicking on the Web ring's logo. Web rings are a great way to visit the Web sites of fellow gardening enthusiasts. You don't need to join a ring in order to surf the Web pages that belong to it. Throughout the book we've listed relevant Web rings. Here are some general gardening ones.

FRIENDS OF THE GARDEN
http://www.virtualseeds.com/ring.html

PLANT PALS WEB RING
http://www.boldweb.com/greenweb/joinweb.htm

THE GARDEN WEB RING
http://cust.iamerica.net/vanessa/gwring.htm

TOWN GARDENS WEB RING
http://www.maigold.co.uk/webring.htm

THE BONSAI WEB RING
http://www.xs4all.nl/~btsmith/BunjinRing/R_members.htm

INDOOR PLANTS WEB RING
http://www.globalnode.com/i_plants

🌿 Gardening Newsgroups

There are many Usenet newsgroups devoted to gardening. Newsgroups tend to be less "clubby" than mailing lists. Some are pretty raucous, since there's no one moderating the discussion. Head to Chapter 1 for directions on how to subscribe to them and read messages through your ISP or AOL.

For a complete guide to the Usenet gardening newsgroups head to **Gardenscape's Newsgroup List** (**http://www.gardenscape.com/GSMagsBooks.html**).

Here are the major newsgroups devoted to gardening.

rec.gardens
rec.gardens.gardening
rec.gardens.orchids
rec.ponds
rec.arts.bonsai
alt.folklore.herbs
rec.gardens.roses
alt.landscape.architecture
rec.gardens.ecosystems
uk.rec.gardening (gardening in the UK)
aus.gardens (gardening in Australia)

👋 **Warning to Parents!** The Usenet newsgroups are unmoderated and uncensored. That means that some of these groups are rife with pornography, ads, and other nasty stuff.

free Gardening Tips & Answers

Great gardens come from little details—the pinch of bone-meal that gets your peonies blooming, the onions that bloom profusely on the dry edge of the walk. Visit these Web sites to read a variety of gardening tips and suggestions, from advice on buying hand trowels to tips for splitting daylilies. There are even Web sites where professional gardeners will try their best to answer your gardening questions.

Free Answers to Gardening Questions

THE NATIONAL GARDENING ASSOCIATION'S QUESTION AND ANSWER
http://www.garden.org/ngaqua/home.asp
E-mail your gardening questions to Charlie Nardozzi, a senior horticulturist at the NGA. He and his staff will try their best to come up with answers in a couple days.

ALL EXPERTS GARDENING Q&A
http://www.allexperts.com/arts/gardening/index.shtml
Expert volunteers will do their best to provide answers to your garden problems.

LINDA GREVEN'S GARDENING ANSWERS
http://www.gdnanswers.com
Linda answers questions about lawn, soil, annuals, perennials, organic gardening, and house plants.

Free Gardening Tips

GARDEN SOLUTIONS—INFODIGGER
http://infodigger.gardensolutions.com/index.html
Type in a word like "bulb" and InfoDigger will search the National Gardening Association's database of more than 17,000 answered questions, 800 gardening tips, and 600 articles to find the information you need.

GET GROWING GARDENING TIPS
http://www.discoveredmonton.com/Devonian/gardtips.html
Dr. Michael Hickman, Associate Director of the University of Alberta's Devonian Botanic Garden, shares a selection of gardening tips from his radio show.

FLOWER AND GARDEN CARE TIPS
http://www.aboutflowers.com/caretips_frame2.html

REBECCA'S GARDEN—GARDEN TIPS
http://www.rebeccasgarden.com/tips/main-list.html

DR. BOB'S GARDENING TIPS
http://hort.ifas.ufl.edu/gt/index.html

HOME HORTICULTURE TIPS
http://www.msue.msu.edu/msue/imp/mod03/master03.html

FREQUENTLY ASKED QUESTIONS ABOUT FLOWERS
http://www.1stinflowers.com/flowerfaqs.html

MINTER'S GARDENING TIPS
http://www.minter.org/list.htm

GET GROWING GARDENING TIPS
http://www.discoveredmonton.com/Devonian/getgro13.html

TIPS AND TECHNIQUES FOR SEED GERMINATION
http://www3.nf.sympatico.ca/angelgrove/SEED.HTM

HELPFUL TIPS FROM PLANTLOVERS.COM
http://www.plantlovers.com/hints/index.html

This page was created by Pam Erikson and Northeast Ent.

Read a variety of tips on birds and flowers in your garden from PlantLovers.Com.

GARDENING TIPS AT YOUR FINGERTIPS
http://www.gardentips.com

IN YOUR GARDEN
TIPS FROM AMERICAN PLANT FOOD COMPANY
http://www.americanplantfood.com/tips.htm

🛒 ROSIE'S WEEKLY TIPS
http://go.flowerlink.com/html/infodir/rosie/rosie.cfm

GARDENING BASICS
http://www.agnr.umd.edu/users/mg/bascont.htm
Learn the basics of gardening from starting with good soil to growing roses.

GREEN THUMB CORNER
http://www.gogrow.com

The Hadley School for the Blind in Winnetka, Illinois offers free couses on gardening for the blind through their Web site (**http://www.hadley-school.org**), including courses on container gardening, bird song identification, and other ways that the visually impaired can enjoy the great outdoors. They're offered in Braille, on cassette, and, in some instances, in large print versions.

free Soil & Lawn Care Help

You can't raise pretty blooms without good soil. All good gardeners start their garden by conditioning its dirt. Is your lawn looking rugged? It may be the soil that's to blame. Tap into these Web sites to learn the basics of soil care, as well as how to diagnose soil problems. We've also included a collection of Web sites that instruct on the fine art of lawn care, from mowing patterns to organic weed control—perfect for that 12-year-old with a mower who's starting his or her lawn-care career.

Free Soil First-Aid

SOIL PH AND FERTILIZERS
http://ext.msstate.edu/pubs/is372.htm
Dr. David Tatum and Keith Crouse of the Mississippi State Extension Service explain soil pH and provide a chart of commonly grown landscape plants and their desired pH ranges.

"WHAT MAKES GOOD GARDEN SOIL?" BY JOHN MERTUS
http://www.mertus.org/gardening/soil.html

"SOIL MANAGEMENT IN YARDS AND GARDENS" BY CRAIG COGGER OF THE WASHINGTON STATE UNIVERSITY EXTENSION
http://gardening.wsu.edu/library/lanb003/lanb003.htm

SOIL GLOSSARY
http://weber.u.washington.edu/~robh/S-7/soilglossary.html
Robert B. Harrison of the University of Washington defines soil terms, starting with abrasion and ending with yard waste.

A COMPENDIUM OF ON-LINE SOIL SURVEY INFORMATION
http://www.itc.nl/%7Erossiter/research/rsrch_ss.html
David G. Rossiter has compiled an incredible resource of worldwide soil information.

Free Lawn Care Help

LAWN WORLD
http://www.lawnworld.com

Tap into an extensive database of lawn-care advice. You'll find links to information on lawn care in specific states, plus weed and tick control advice.

LAWN CARE FOR HOMEOWNERS
http://www.oznet.ksu.edu/dp_hfrr/TURF/HOME.htm
*Kansas State University offers lawn-care advice. You'll need the free Adobe Acrobat browser plug-in (**http://www.adobe.com**) to read the pamphlets.*

ORGANIC LAWN CARE FROM WHITNEY FARMS
http://www.whitneyfarm.com/garden/geninfo/lawn_main.html
Learn how to feed your soil the healthy way.

Soil Help
University extension services provide invaluable advice on diagnosing and solving local soil woes. Head to Chapter 22 for links to the major extension service Web sites and help on finding an extension service in your community.

ORGANIC LAWN CARE FOR THE CHEAP AND LAZY FROM PAUL WHEATON
http://www.split.com/lawn
Does this sound great, or what?

COOL SEASON GRASSES: LAWN ESTABLISHMENT AND RENOVATION
http://muextension.missouri.edu/xplor/agguides/hort/g06700.htm
John H. Dunn and Brad S. Fresenburg of the University of Missouri-Columbia Extension Service explain how to grow turf grass.

LEAST TOXIC WAYS TO CONTROL WEEDS AND LAWNS
http://www.metrokc.gov/hazwaste/house/garden/controlweed lawn.html
Learn how to use clippings, organic fertilizer, aeration, and over-seeding techniques, courtesy of the Local Hazardous Waste Management Program of Seattle, Washington.

HOME LAWN WEED CONTROL
http://muextension.missouri.edu/xplor/agguides/hort/g06750.htm
Brad S. Fresenburg, John H. Dunn, and Erik H. Ervin of the University of Missouri-Columbia Extension Service offer advice on weed eradication.

"YOUR LAWN'S 25 WORST WEED ENEMIES" FROM THE DELAWARE COOPERATIVE EXTENSION
http://bluehen.ags.udel.edu/deces/hyg/hyg-45.html

HOMETIME'S LAWN HOW-TO CENTER
http://www.pbs.org/hometime/pc/lg/pc2lglaw.htm
Learn how to seed, sod, aerate, water, and more.

LAWN TALK FROM THE UNIVERSITY OF ILLINOIS EXTENSION
http://www.urbanext.uiuc.edu/lawntalk/lawntalk08.html
Planting a new lawn, rejuvenating an old one, and weed control are among the many lawn-care topics addressed.

Get Drought Help on the Web
Learn how to keep your lawn and garden healthy during droughts at **Water Wise Gardening** (**http://www.ebmud.com/watercon/garden.html**). This site offers valuable advice on steps you can take to nurture your yard and still save water.

TURF TIPS FROM PURDUE UNIVERSITY
http://www.agry.purdue.edu/turf/tips/index.html
New tips are added weekly to this lawn-care Web site.

LAWN & GARDEN FROM THE UNIVERSITY OF SASKATCHEWAN
http://pine.usask.ca/cofa/departments/hort/hortinfo/yards/index.html
You'll find a wide variety of articles on lawn care, fertilization, and clean up.

MOWING YOUR LAWN
http://www.cahe.nmsu.edu/pubs/_h/h-505.html
Lynn Ellen Doxon, a horticulturist at New Mexico State University, explains how to determine the proper height for your lawn, how often to mow it, what to do with clippings, and more.

PROPER LAWN MOWING
http://www.msue.msu.edu/msue/imp/mod03/01701019.html
This article from Michigan State University Extension explains how the height of your lawn and how often you mow it will effect how healthy it looks.

THATCH AND ITS CONTROL
http://bluehen.ags.udel.edu/deces/hyg/hyg-41.html
Is thatch good or bad? This article from the Delaware Cooperative Extension explains how a thin layer can be beneficial to lawns.

 Help for Organic Gardeners

You don't need pesticides and artificial fertilizers to grow great vegetables and beautiful flowers. That's the philosophy behind organic gardening. Instead you rely on natural nutrients, the keystone of your campaign being your compost pile. Whether you're a hardcore "vegan-ecotarian" or you (like our husbands) occasionally lapse from a lofty organic credo and sneak out in the middle of the night to spray Miracle Grow on the tomatoes, there's a Web site out there that will help both you and your compost pile achieve greater oneness with Mother Earth.

You can chat with other organic gardeners in the Usenet newsgroup **rec.gardens.ecosystems**. *Head to Chapter 1 for directions on subscribing to the newsgroup with your Web browser.*

Basic Organic Gardening Advice

ORGANIC GROWERS
http://www.organic-growers.com

THE GARDEN SPOT BY MORT MATHER
http://supak.com/mort/default.htm
Lots of answers to your organic gardening questions, plus several online columns.

HOWARD GARETT'S BASIC ORGANIC PROGRAM
http://www.dirtdoctor.com
*Howard Garett, also known as The Dirt Doctor, offers articles and a link to his radio show. You can listen to the latter live on the Web if you have the free browser plug-in RealAudio (*http://www.real.com*).*

🛒 ORGANIC GARDENING FROM THE GREEN WEB
http://www.boldweb.com/greenweb/organic.htm

ORGANIC GARDENING MAGAZINE
http://www.organicgardening.com

What does it mean to be an organic gardener? It means that you put back into the earth as much as—or more than—you take out. Learn how to create an organic garden, from developing rich soil to growing healthy plants without pesticides or fungicides.

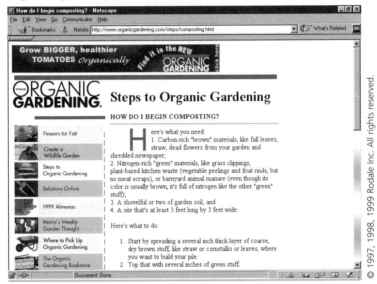

Learn how to start your organic garden at the Web site of Organic Gardening Magazine.

ORGANIC GROWING FROM DOWN UNDER
http://www.organicdownunder.com

ROD'S ORGANIC VEGGIE PATCH
http://www.ozemail.com.au/~cynos

ORGANIC GROWING
http://www.organic-growers.com
The Canberra, Australia Organic Growers Society hosts a question and answer section.

CANADIAN ORGANIC GROWERS
http://www.gks.com/cog/index.html

This Web page was created by David Heaton

David & Kay Heaton's site offers lots of advice on growing veggies without chemicals.

ELIZABETH AND CROW'S AWESOME ORGANIC CYBER GARDEN
http://www.vcity.net/cybergarden
Tap into the marvelous Web site of gardening authors and organic gardening experts Elizabeth and Crow Miller's for articles, features, and insights. Article topics include "How to Have a 100 Percent Organic Lawn Maintenance Business" and "Organic Golf Courses."

🍃 Free Composting Help

HOW TO COMPOST
http://net.indra.com/~topsoil/How_to_Compost.html
Eric S. Johnson explains how to tell if compost is ready to be worked into your garden, how to use compost, and how compost benefits the soil.

BACKYARD MAGIC: THE COMPOSTING HANDBOOK
http://www.gov.nb.ca/environm/comucate/compost/magic.htm
The New Brunswick, Canada, Department of the Environment tells you everything you need to know to get started composting.

COMPOSTING INSTRUCTION SHEETS
http://www.rco.on.ca/factsheet/fs_e03.html
The Recycling Council of Ontario tells you how to compost in wood and wire bins or rotating barrel composters, and offers tips on topics like making leaves work for you.

THE COMPOST RESOURCE PAGE
http://www.oldgrowth.org/compost

MASTER COMPOSTER
http://www.mastercomposter.com
Select a region and the Master Composter Web site will help you find a composting program in your area. Master Composter also offers extensive instructions and reference materials.

COMPOSTING WITH RED WIGGLER WORMS
http://www.cityfarmer.org/wormcomp61.html#wormcompost
Gillian Elcock and Josie Martens of City Farmer, from Canada's Office of Urban Agriculture, explain how to get you and your worms working together at composting organic household waste.

Free Help with Organic Fertilizing and Pest Control

NATIONAL GARDENING ASSOCIATION: ORGANIC FERTILIZERS
http://www2.garden.org/nga/EDIT/Articles/orgfert.qua

Synthetic fertilizers are manufactured, while organic ones come from plants and animals. Learn how to select and apply organic fertilizers in this wonderful tutorial.

SAFER GARDENING AND PEST CONTROL
http://www.metrokc.gov/hazwaste/house/pests.html

Steps to a healthy pesticide-free garden, and how to use bugs to control bugs are the topics at this illuminating Web site from the Local Hazardous Waste Management Program in Seattle, Washington.

PESTICIDE EDUCATION CENTER
http://www.igc.apc.org/pesticides/index.html

The Pesticide Education Center is a non-profit organization founded in 1988 to educate the public about the hazards of pesticides to human health and the environment.

free Greenhouse Building & Growing Advice

S ome of us would rather own a greenhouse than a house to live in, but you don't need to spring for a mortgage on two homes to enjoy growing plants year-round. Find out how to build your own greenhouse with low-cost supplies like PVC on these Web sites.

A SMALL BACKYARD GREENHOUSE FOR THE HOME GARDENER
http://www.bae.ncsu.edu/programs/extension/publicat/postharv/gr een/green.html
Learn how to build an inexpensive greenhouse with PVC pipe at this Web site from the North Carolina Cooperative Extension.

TEXAS MANAGEMENT GREENHOUSE HANDBOOK
http://aggie-horticulture.tamu.edu/greenhouse/guides/green/ green.html
This extensive online handbook is based on a publication by Dr. Don Wilkerson of the Texas Agricultural Extension Service. You'll learn about greenhouse structures, heating requirements, irrigation, and more. A resource list is included.

HOBBY GREENHOUSE ASSOCIATION
http://www.orbitworld.net/hga
Hobby Greenhouse is a non-profit group for people who enjoy growing plants year-round in greenhouses.

Take a Virtual Tour of the University of Georgia's Greenhouses
(**http://dogwood.botany.uga.edu/Tour.html**) View ferns, cycads, unique gymnosperms, arid plants, tropical plants, and carnivorous plants.

PLANNING AND BUILDING A GREENHOUSE FROM THE WEST VIRGINIA UNIVERSITY EXTENSION SERVICE
http://www.wvu.edu/~agexten/hortcult/greenhou/building.htm

 GREENHOUSE CONSTRUCTION TIPS
http://www.charleysgreenhouse.com/5tech_tips.htm
Courtesy of Charley's Greenhouses, learn tips on topics like building your greenhouse foundation.

SHERRY'S GREENHOUSE
http://www.sherrysgreenhouse.com
Sherry tells you about her greenhouse and answers greenhouse questions.

Looking for Greenhouse Supplies?
Check out Charley's Greenhouses
(**http://www.charleysgreenhouse.com**) and Sundance Supply (**http://www.sundancesupply.com**).

free Help Growing Flowers

It's happened to all of us at some time: we've purchased a seed packet with dreams of growing the flower garden pictured on the packet. What comes out of the dirt is something entirely different and almost invariably disappointing. Meanwhile, Grandma or Aunt Milly seems to grow, nearly effortlessly, half-acres blanketed by blooms over which clouds of butterflies flutter.

For help growing annuals we suggest heading to the big gardening Web sites we recommend in Chapter 2. Many offer advice on nurturing specific annuals.

Then head to the **National Gardening Association** (**http://www.garden.org/edit/search.asp**) Web site and search their article database by typing "petunia," "geranium," or even "butterfly garden" for articles on those blooms from the association's magazine.

For help selecting the proper flower, head to **Better Homes & Garden's Editor's Choice Plant Guide** (**http://www.bhg.com/gardening**). You can search it by plant type, hardiness, zone, and lighting, for editors' picks of best varieties to grow.

Finally, the **University of Nebraska–Lincoln Cooperative Extension** offers an excellent Guide to Growing Annual Flowers on its Web site (**http://www.ianr.unl.edu/pubs/Horticulture/g721.htm**).

Note: You'll find Web sites that offer help with perennials in the next chapter.

T I P

Looking for Recipes to Dry Flowers?
Head to the flower drying tutorial on **Learn2.Com** (**http://learn2.com/08/0826/0826.html**). There's also a tutorial on making potpourri (**http://learn2.com/05/0559/0559.html**). Find more flower craft ideas at **Garden Web's Flower & Craft Forum** (**http://www.gardenweb.com/forums/crafts**). Rebecca's Garden (**http://www.rebeccasgarden.com**) also offers regular flower crafting projects and help.

 *Free Help Growing Bulbs*

GROWING COLORS HOME AND GARDEN
http://www.growingcolors.com

Tap into this bulb reference guide for help on spring and fall plantings, bulb forcing, and container growing. You can search the guide by criteria such as bloom time, height, sun exposure, indoor forcing capacity, and many more for recommendations.

BULB TIPS FROM SOUTHERN LIVING ONLINE
http://southernliving.com/garden/bulbs.html

BETTER HOMES & GARDENS
GUIDE TO SPRING BULBS
http://www.bhg.com/gardening

 THE INTERNATIONAL BULB SOCIETY
http://www.bulbsociety.com/index.html

THE INTERNATIONAL BULB SOCIETY DISCUSSION BOARDS
http://www.bulbsociety.com/Discus
Learn all about bulbs—when to buy them, how to plant them, and bulb conservation.

THE GEOPHYTE PAGE BY DR. WILLIAM B. MILLER OF CLEMSON UNIVERSITY

http://virtual.clemson.edu/groups/hort/sctop/geophyte/webpage.htm

Information on bulbs, corms, tubers, and other geophytic plants.

AMERICAN DAFFODIL SOCIETY

http://www.mc.edu/~adswww

This Web page was created by Nancy Tackett.

Help for growing these sunny flowers, plus instructions for subscribing to DAFNET, a forum about growing and hybridizing daffodils.

 VAN BOURGONDIEN DUTCH BULBS

http://www.dutchbulbs.com

Articles from The Bulb Lady, *along with* The Bulb Lady's Garden Guide, *featuring bulb and tubers dos and don'ts.*

 HOLLAND FLOWERBULB COMPANY

http://www.hfc-flowerbulbs.nl/index2.html

Gardening tips include how to make a garden plan, planting tulips in flower boxes, and forcing bulbs.

AMARYLLIS—A POPULAR GIFT

http://www.familygardening.com/gdinfo36.html

Family Gardening offers a great article on forcing amaryllis bulbs to create a beautiful winter gift.

BULB.COM
http://www.bulb.com

The U.S. Netherlands Flower Bulb Information Center (NFBIC) is the U.S. press office of the Dutch flower bulb industry. Although geared to the press, the extensive information will delight any bulb grower.

ALPINES AND BULBS DISCUSSION GROUP
http://www.suite101.com/discussions.cfm/alpines_and_bulbs
Hosted by Gary Buckley at Suite 101.Com, this is the place to find out why none of the bulbs you planted last fall bloomed.

PLANT IDEAS—INDOOR CULTURE BULBS
http://www.plantideas.com/bulb/indexbulb.html
Plantideas.com offers tips on growing bulbs indoors and out. You can find information on over thirty kinds of flowers: hardy bulbs such as tulips, crocus, and hyacinth, or tender bulbs such as cyclamen, freesia, or fairy lilies.

FREESIA HOMEPAGE
http://www.flowerinfo.nl/freesia/index.html

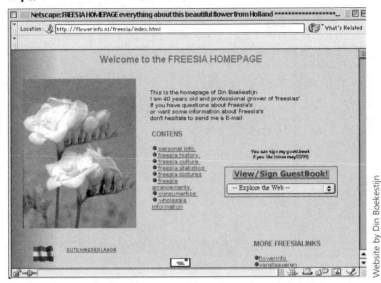

Din Boekestijn, a professional freesia grower, shares his tips.

 Free Help Growing Dahlias

THE ONLINE GUIDE TO GROWING DAHLIAS
http://sashimi.wwa.com/~jjf/dahlia.html

Joe and Mindy share lots of great info on growing perfect dahlias. We especially appreciate that they've included printable instructions. There's also a forum area where you can post your dahlia questions.

"GROWING DAHLIAS" FROM THE COOPERATIVE EXTENSION, UNIVERSITY OF NEBRASKA-LINCOLN
http://www.ianr.unl.edu/pubs/Horticulture/g189.htm

THE AMERICAN DAHLIA SOCIETY
http://www.dahlia.com

You'll find lots of links to Web resources, plus information on joining several dahlia mailing lists.

Free Help Growing Daylilies

THE DAYLILY EXCHANGE
http://www.daylily.com

Michael Longo hosts this Web site, which includes a huge listing of daylily advice pages around the Net.

© Michael Longo, 1996, 1997, 1998, 1999.

 THE DAYLILY PLACE
http://www.a1.com/daylily/place.html

The homepage for the Daylily E-mail Round Robin, a group of members of the American Hemerocallis Society who share their experiences and ideas about daylilies. You'll find poll results such as their top ten picks for daylilies under $10, lots of photos, and plenty of tips.

DAYLILIES ALONG THE INFORMATION HIGHWAY
http://www.daylilies.com/daylilies

 **Take a Virtual Tour of Monet's Garden!** Tap into the online home tour of Monet's house and garden in Giverny, France (**http://www.giverny.org/gardens**) to see the gardens that inspired Monet. There's even a map of the garden, a list of plants, and growing tips.

AMERICAN HEMEROCALLIS SOCIETY
http://www.daylilies.org/daylilies.html
Membership information, plus answers to common questions such as: "Why is the daylily the perfect perennial?"

FRIENDS OF THE DAYLILY
http://www.primenet.com/~tjfehr/daylily.html
This FAQ page from Tim Fehr and The Friends of the Daylilies tells you everything you need to know to grow perfect blooms—and keep them blooming.

If you need to cling tight to a few blooming violets in order to get through a bleak winter, check out **African Violets Online** (**http://avsa.org**). Get blooming tips and find out about the latest hot African violet varieties.

Free Help Growing Irises

WORLD IRIS ASSOCIATION
http://www.worldiris.com
Stop in at the cyberhome of the World Iris Association and The Historic Iris Preservation Society.

THE AMERICAN IRIS SOCIETY
http://www.irises.org
Learn how to grow and care for irises, view photos, and learn about e-mail lists and chat groups devoted to iris discussion.

HOME PAGE FOR IRISES
http://aleph0.clarku.edu/~djoyce/iris
David Pane-Joyce's site includes lots of links to other iris resources on the Web.

Free Help Growing Other Flowers

"GROWING GLADIOLUS"
BY AMY J. GREVING, THE UNIVERSITY OF
NEBRASKA–LINCOLN COOPERATIVE EXTENSION
http://www.ianr.unl.edu/pubs/Horticulture/g852.htm

PEONIES FOR THE HOME LANDSCAPE
http://www.ces.ncsu.edu/hil/hil-8501.html
Erv Evans of the North Carolina State University provides a basic primer on choosing, planting, and caring for your peonies.

EMILY'S SUNFLOWER GARDEN
http://members.xoom.com/MySunflowers
Emily Christensen offers advice and inspiration on growing the festive sunflower—as well as recipes for sunflower seed treats.

FIVE EASY STEPS TO A SUCCESSFUL
WILDFLOWER GARDEN OR MEADOW
http://www.earthlygoods.com/questionanswer.html
Earthly Goods tells you how to plant a wildflower garden for which neighborhood birds and butterflies will thank you.

THE LANGUAGE OF FLOWERS
http://vbcgold.com/lang.htm
Did you know that the Aster is a symbol of love? Twigs offers a guide to the meanings associated with flowers.

MARY'S GARDENS
http://www.mgardens.org
Mary's Gardens is a 50-year-old Philadelphia organization devoted to studying the symbolism of flowers in medieval art as they relate to the Virgin Mary, and also to growing and planning flower gardens devoted to the religious spirit.

Peruse a rare 1637 tulip catalog from 17th century nurseryman P. Cos of Haarlem, Holland at **http://www.bib.wau.nl/tulips.**

free Help Growing Perennials

They grow stronger and more beautiful each year. That's part of the magic of perennials. They fold into a landscape effortlessly and transform it into a storybook garden with delicate color. The trick of growing perennials is selecting the ones best suited to your climate and locale. There are lots of Web sites that will help. Here are our favorites:

PERRY'S PERENNIAL PAGES
http://moose.uvm.edu/~pass/perry
*We guarantee that perennial lovers who tap into the Web site of Dr. Leonard Perry, a professor at the University of Vermont, will not surface for hours. There are links to hundreds of extension service pamphlets and Web resources devoted to selecting and growing perennials in just about every part of the country, plus hundreds of articles on perennials. You can watch slide shows about perennials and listen to perennial-related radio broadcasts, assuming you have the browser plug-in RealAudio (**http://www.realaudio.com**) installed. You can search an A-Z database of perennials with photos and growing advice. There's even fun stuff like a Perennial Arcade with quizzes, games, and crossword puzzles to test your perennial knowledge.*

ETERA
http://www.etera.com
You'll find a searchable database of thousands of perennial gardening articles and a helpful FAQ. There are also free electronic greeting cards to send and a screensaver to download.

WISEACRE GARDENS
http://www.wiseacre-gardens.com/plants/photo/buglew.html
A perennial and wildflower photo gallery with brief descriptions. There's an assortment of Windows wallpaper to download and virtual postcards to send.

🛒 HERITAGE PERENNIALS
http://www.perennials.com

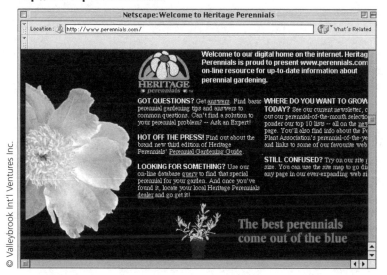

Basic perennial gardening tips on topics like selecting and planting perennials, perennials in the shade, and gardening with ornamental grasses, plus answers to common questions such as: "When is the best time to plant?"

🛒 PERENNIAL TUTORIAL 101 FROM BUDS (FINE PERENNIALS & BULBS)
http://www.budsgarden.com/startup.html
Learn to build a perennial garden, the basics of bulb planting, and what the symbols on plant tags mean.

PERENNIALS
http://www.ces.ncsu.edu/depts/hort/consumer/perennials/Perenni.htm
Search this alphabetized listing of perennials, from Dr. Alice B. Russell, Department of Horticultural Science, North Carolina State University, by common name or scientific name for descriptions and photos.

TUBA'S FABULOUS PERENNIALS
http://members.aol.com/Tubablues/Index.html
Click on "perennial lists" and "featured articles" and you'll be pleasantly surprised by the amount of perennial information packed into this site.

PERENNIAL WEB
http://www.perennialweb.com

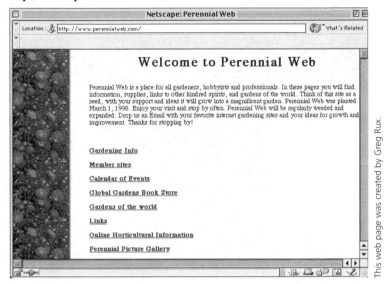

This web page was created by Greg Rux.

View pictures and read articles like "Northern Day Lily Culture" and "Soil Structure in the Culture of Hosta" at this growing site that includes links to gardens of the world and more.

THE PERENNIAL GARDENER WITH KAREN STROHBEEN
http://www.pbs.org/perennialgardener
Learn about this PBS show, read gardening tips, view plant features, and download some free garden desktop art.

THE CARE AND MAINTENANCE OF PERENNIALS FROM THE NEW YORK BOTANICAL GARDENS
http://www.nybg.org/gardens/pcare.html

PERENNIAL PLANT ASSOCIATION
http://www.perennialplant.org

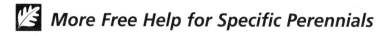 *More Free Help for Specific Perennials*

THE AMERICAN HOSTA SOCIETY
http://www.hosta.org

IAN'S CHRYSANTHEMUM PAGE
http://web.ukonline.co.uk/i.payne/index.html

THE NATIONAL CHRYSANTHEMUM SOCIETY
http://www.mums.org

BILL'S FUCHSIA SITE
http://www.harbornet.com/folks/tyler/index.html

free Help Growing Roses

"I never promised you a rose garden," the song goes, but why wait for someone else to grow your rose bower? Rose growing is addictive. And roses are not as hard to cultivate as one might believe. A well-drained sunny spot and a little attention with the garden hose and pruning sheers are about all that's needed to grow a bush of blooms so timeless in their elegance you'll wonder why you ever waited for someone else to give you a bouquet of them. Rose lovers are everywhere on the Web, sharing advice and pictures of their gardens. Here's how to join them:

THE ROSES PAGE
http://www.mc.edu/~nettles/rofaq/rofaq-top.html

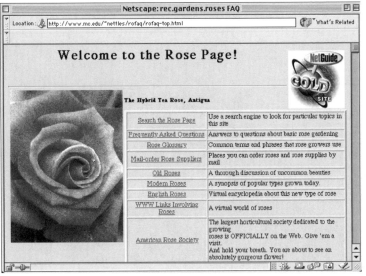

Page hosted by Bill Nettles

The Roses Page offers a compilation of questions and answers about roses that appeared in the Usenet Newsgroup rec.gardens.roses. You'll find a rose glossary, a list of mail-order suppliers, information on old roses, modern roses, and English roses, plus lots of links to rose growing resources around the Web.

Looking for a Special Rose Variety?
Head to the **Search Lists List of Roses** (**http://www.helpmefind.com/sites/rrr/sltlist.html**). You can search for roses by name, class or color. You can also see pictures of some of the roses.

ROSES AT ABOUT.COM
http://roses.about.com
Ted Bissland is your host for weekly features, a free newsletter, a rose chat, and all types of rose-related links at this wonderful site.

 TIMELESS ROSES
http://www.timelessroses.com
Learn how to care for roses, including the basics like feeding, winterizing, pruning, cutting, and controlling blackspot.

 YESTERDAY'S ROSE
http://www.Country-Lane.com/yr
Old-fashioned roses are the subject of this beautiful site.

THE ROSE GARDEN BY WENDY RONALD
http://gardens.co.nz/RoseGarden/index.html

This web page by Wendy Ronald

View photos of roses from around the world.

LADY JAI'S ROSES
http://members.visi.net/~jai
You'll read about how to prune, winterize, and propagate roses, plus read articles on different varieties of roses and more at this homey site.

DONNA'S ROSES IN THE SHADE PAGE
http://www.nbn.com/~holmes/roses.htm
Donna explains that it is possible, suggests varieties, and gives nurturing advice.

THE TEXAS ROSE RUSTLERS
http://www.texas-rose-rustlers.com
Learn about this group of old rose enthusiasts from Central Texas that searches for surviving old rose specimens in older communities.

ROOTING ROSES IN A BAGGIE FROM THE AMERICAN ROSE SOCIETY
http://www.ars.org/experts/roserooting.html
Mel Hulse explains how it's done.

PRUNING ROSES
FROM THE AMERICAN ROSE SOCIETY
http://www.ars.org/experts/prunemenu.html
Tap into the American Rose Society's Web site for numerous articles on pruning roses, including ones on pruning back older roses and the trepidation of pruning.

SHOW ROSES AND EXHIBITING
http://hometown.aol.com/DugDbold/index.html
Doug Diebold and Rachel Hunter tell you what you need to know to jump into the world of exhibiting prized roses. They tell you how to transport and groom your roses and how roses are judged.

FREQUENTLY ASKED QUESTIONS ABOUT ROSES BY BILL CHANDLE
http://www.mc.edu/~nettles/rofaq/rofaq-faq.html#FAQ_qa_propagate

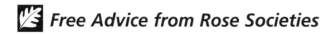 *Free Advice from Rose Societies*

WORLD FEDERATION OF ROSE SOCIETIES
http://www.worldrose.org
The WFRS is an association of the national rose societies in 34 countries.

Read news of rose breeding around the world at the Web site of the World Federation of Rose Societies.

CANADIAN ROSE SOCIETY
http://www.mirror.org/groups/crs
You'll find beautiful photos, advice on planting and care of roses in Canadian climates, and a weekly rose chat where you can talk to other rose lovers.

ROSES IN OYAMA
http://www.asahi-net.or.jp/~nv1h-ymgc/index-e.html
This is an English language page with a link to The Oyama Rose Society in Japan.

HERITAGE ROSE FOUNDATION
http://www.gardenweb.com/directory/chs/
Get information about the world congress on heritage roses.

THE AMERICAN ROSE SOCIETY
http://www.ars.org
The Web site of the ARS is loaded with information on all aspects of rose care. Head to the Ask the Experts section for good advice on everything from arranging rose to planting companion plants.

The American Rose Society offers regular features on nurturing, pruning, and wintering roses. The Rose of the Month feature profiles of exciting new varieties of roses.

ROYAL NATIONAL ROSE SOCIETY
http://www.roses.co.uk/harkness/rnrs/rnrs.htm

LOCAL AND DISTRICT ROSE SOCIETIES
http://www.ars.org/localsoc.html
The American Rose Society has over 400 local societies. This site details local chapters who have their own Web sites.

THE ROSE RESOURCE
BY THE ALL-AMERICAN ROSE SELECTION
http://www.rose.org

The AARS is a non-profit group of rose growers dedicated to rose research and promotion. Tap into their Web site to read tips about rose gardening, designing with roses, and culturing prize-winning roses.

Tap into the Web site of the All-American Rose Selections to learn about public rose gardens in your area or the spot that you're traveling to.

Rose Photography
Photographing roses well is as much of an art as growing them. For hints on getting better pictures, read an interview with professional rose photographer Bonnie Andrews at **California Photographer** (**http://calphoto.com/roses.htm**).

Chat With Other Rose Lovers in Forums and Newsgroups

If you'd like to discuss rose gardening with other rose lovers, check out the discussions on the following Web sites.

ROSE FORUMS FROM THE GARDEN WEB
http://www.gardenweb.com/forums/rosesind
You'll find discussions for everything from rose propagation and exchange to organic rose growing, roses in Oz, and European growing.

THE ANTIQUE ROSE ADVISOR
The Antique Rose Advisor hosts two large message boards devoted to rose fandom. (One board became too large and a second board was created.)

• *ASK THE ANTIQUE ROSE ADVISOR (1)*
http://www.sonic.net/webgrafix/roseboard

• *ASK THE ANTIQUE ROSE ADVISOR (2)*
http://www.sonic.net/webgrafix/roseboard2

To chit-chat with rose growers around the world through the Usenet newsgroups, set your browser to subscribe to the **rec.gardens.roses** newsgroup. (Head to Chapter 1 for directions on how to do it.)

Send a Virtual Rose!
At The Internet Rose (**http://www.theinternetrose.com**), you can send a free virtual rose greeting to one you love.

Or, Visit A Virtual Rose Garden

A TOUR OF MY ROSE GARDEN
http://www.playground.net/~thompson

Surf the Web Pages of Other Rose Lovers

To visit the Web sites of fellow rose lovers, surf these "rings." A ring is a linked group of Web sites. To surf the ring, you click the logo to hop from one Web site to the next. You don't have to join the ring to travel it.

THE ANTIQUE ROSE WEB RING
http://icdweb.cc.purdue.edu/~aquila/arose.html
Scroll to the bottom of the page and select "list sites" to view more rose Web pages.

THE PERFECT ROSE WEB RING
http://www.themustangs.com/sabrinasworld/perfectrose
Follow this web ring to see more rose Web pages.

If your local nursery doesn't have what you're looking for, visit the Web sites of these mail order rose dealers:

EDMUND'S ROSES
http://www.edmundsroses.com

JACKSON & PERKINS
http://www.jackson-perkins.com

WHITE RABBIT ROSES
http://www.mcn.org/b/roses

MICHAEL'S PREMIERE ROSES
http://www.michaelsrose.com

LIGGETT'S ROSE NURSERY
http://www.liggettroses.com

GARDEN SOLUTIONS
http://www.gardensolutions.com

free Help Growing Vegetables

Everyone loves fresh veggies—most people, anyhow. A bag full from the garden is a quick way to endear oneself to relatives and neighbors. Even dogs appreciate fresh produce, as Judy discovered when a hound she adopted from the pound quickly mimicked her habit of plucking cherry tomatoes off plants and swallowing them. She soon found him eating his way down garden rows, chomping tomatoes, strawberries, and whatever else he could pluck from the leaves. He went on to show the neighbor's dog how to harvest veggies. The two dogs blithely chomped their way through Judy's garden as well as that of her neighbors. Shortly after, the neighbors returned their dog to its breeder. They complained, "He kept eating tomatoes in Grandma's garden. We couldn't keep a dog who did that." Vegetable gardening is best when it's a family affair. That means sharing your tomatoes with friends and neighbors, and your dog, too.

VEGETABLE GUIDE FROM GARDENGUIDES
http://www.gardenguides.com/Vegetables/vegetabl.htm
Dealing with animals in your organic garden (both the invited and the not-invited kind) is one of the many articles on vegetable growing you'll find at this site. There's also lots of help for growing tomatoes.

AMES GARDENING—GROWING VEGETABLES
http://www.ames.com/guides/veggies/index.html
Good advice on soil, tomatoes, other veggies, and tools.

  Chat About Your Vegetable Garden Head to the **Vegetable Gardening Forum on the Garden Web** (**http://www.gardenweb.com/forums/cornucop**) to join other gardeners in bulletin board-style chats about gardening.

THE VEGETABLE PATCH
http://www.netspace.net.au/~atkinson/index.htm

Gavin & Paula Atkinson of Brisbane, Australia offer advice for the beginning organic vegetable gardener. They also offer feature articles, vegetable profiles, and a cyber gardening tour.

GROWING VEGETABLES IN THE HOME GARDEN
http://www.hoptechno.com/book26.htm
Advice from Robert Wester and August Kehr of the United States Department of Agriculture.

SITES FOR VEGETABLE GARDENS
http://www.msue.msu.edu/msue/imp/mod03/01701337.html
The folks at the Michigan State University Extension offer advice on choosing a garden location, proper spacing of plants, and planting techniques.

ORGANIC VEGETABLE GARDENING
http://edis.ifas.ufl.edu/scripts/htmlgen.exe?DOCUMENT_VH019
James M. Stephens of the University of Florida Cooperative Extension explains that good vegetables are never accidental and discusses the benefits of organic vegetable gardening.

VEGETABLE GARDENING HANDBOOK

http://edis.ifas.ufl.edu/scripts/htmlgen.exe?MENU_VH:VH

The University of Florida Cooperative Extension offers a virtual handbook of veggie gardening help.

"GROWING VEGETABLE TRANSPLANTS FOR THE HOME GARDEN" BY LARRY BASS

http://www.ces.ncsu.edu/depts/hort/hil/hil-8104.html
http://www.ces.ncsu.edu/depts/hort/hil/hil-8104.html

VEGETABLE INFORMATION FROM AGGIE HORTICULTURE

http://aggie-horticulture.tamu.edu/PLANTanswers/vegetables/veg.html

From the Texas Horticulture Program comes an alphabetical index to vegetables, plus help for fungi and insects common to them.

"HORTICULTURE SOLUTIONS FOR VEGETABLES" BY ANGELICA YAMS, THE UNIVERSITY OF ILLINOIS EXTENSION

http://www.ag.uiuc.edu/~robsond/solutions/horticulture/veggies.html

GROWING COMMERCIAL VEGETABLES FROM THE NORTH CAROLINA COOPERATIVE EXTENSION

http://www.ces.ncsu.edu/depts/hort/hil/veg-index.html

You can read online leaflets about growing many different types of vegetables, including Jerusalem artichokes, beets, southern peas, radishes, pumpkins, and winter squash.

Free Help for Growing Tomatoes, Corn, and Strawberries

THE ONLINE TOMATO VINE
http://tomato.vbutler.com

Hey tomato lovers! Here's an entire Web site devoted to discussions on the virtue of Beefsteak versus Fat Boy.

TOMATO TIPS
http://www.tomato.org/tips-pgs/tips.htm

© 1999 California Tomatoes.

Learn about the cancer prevention properties of tomatoes, print recipes for tomatoes, and learn tomato storage tips at the Web site of the California Tomato Commission.

THE TOMATO PLANT PROBLEMS FAQ BY KAY KLIER
http://is.rice.edu/~shel/tomato.html

MR. TOMATO: THE GARDENING INNOVATORS
http://www.mrtomato.com

Read tomato growing tips, FAQs, and other helpful advice.

KINGCORN.ORG FROM PURDUE UNIVERSITY
http://www.agry.purdue.edu/ext/corn

Sweet corn fanatics will love this site, which has features and information on every possible aspect of growing corn, including a searchable database of advice. Corn Culture includes links to other corny wisdom, corny recipes, and stuff made with corn. There also links to corn experts.

THE STRAWBERRIES FACT PAGE
http://www.jamm.com/strawberry/facts.html

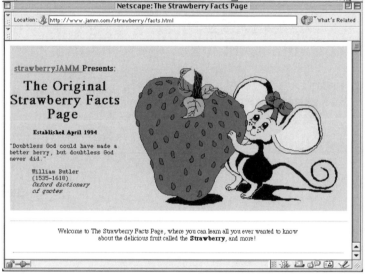

What a fun site! Jenni A. M. Merrifield tells you all you need to know about strawberries (Judy's dog's favorite snack), including gardening tips, recipes, and information about strawberry festivals around the world.

free Help Growing Herbs & Spices

Many fine restaurants grow their own herbs. Why shouldn't you? Dishes spiced with fresh herbs taste so much finer than those cooked with the dried stuff. Herbs aren't hard to grow either. A patch of dirt outside your kitchen door or a few pots on the sill are all you need to get started giving your cooking a whole new taste.

ALGY'S HERB PAGE
http://www.algy.com/herb/index.html
Apothecary and growing herbs in greenhouses are among the topics discussed in Algy's forums. You'll find recipes in the Kitchen link.

CULINARY HERB FAQS
http://metalab.unc.edu/herbmed/culiherb.html
All you ever wanted to know about culinary herbs, including processing them and using them in crafts and potpourri, compiled from discussions in the newsgroups **rec.gardens** *and* **alt.folklore.herbs** *and the Herblist mailing list.*

 ### HERB GUIDE FROM GARDENGUIDES
http://www.gardenguides.com/herbs/herb.htm
Read articles like "You're a Budding Herbalist" and "Echinacea: More Than a Pretty Flower." Learn which herbs are easy to grow in a windowsill garden and which are good for your hair.

HERB DIRECTORY
FROM PENNSYLVANIA STATE UNIVERSITY
http://hortweb.cas.psu.edu/vegcrops/herbs.html
A directory of over 60 commonly grown herbs with information on using and harvesting them.

"SAVORY HERBS CULTURE AND USES" FROM THE USDA
http://www.hort.purdue.edu/newcrop/SavoryHerbs/SavoryHerbs.html

HERB PERENNIALS
http://www.mountainvalleygrowers.com
Sign up for the Herbal Newsletter, *read past issues, and ask herb questions. You'll find lots of good tips such as, "When you work around your lemon grass plants, be sure to wear long sleeves. The blades are extremely sharp and can slice you to ribbons."*

"HERBS AND HERB GARDENING: AN ANNOTATED BIBLIOGRAPHY AND RESOURCE GUIDE" BY SUZANNE DEMUTH OF THE USDA
http://www.nal.usda.gov/afsic/AFSIC_pubs/srb9606.htm

A GUIDE TO MEDICINAL AND AROMATIC PLANTS FROM PURDUE UNIVERSITY
http://www.hort.purdue.edu/newcrop/med-aro/default.html

GERNET KATZER'S SPICE PAGE
http://www-ang.kfunigraz.ac.at/~katzer/engl/index.html
Information on over a hundred spice plants with an emphasis on their use in Asian foods.

Herb Recipe Rescue
Some recipes in modern cookbooks are formulated for dried herbs, some for fresh herbs. Sometimes it's hard to tell whether the author intended 5 tablespoons of dried dill or 5 tablespoons of fresh dill. (Judy once ended up with a pot of green goo instead of soup by misunderstanding the author's intent.) Use caution when substituting fresh for dried, and vice versa.

---

free Help Planting & Caring for Trees

Life is more pleasant in the company of trees. But like any other plant, trees need to be properly cared for or else they'll fall victim to disease, bugs, or an early death. You can often obtain free advice on caring for an ailing tree by calling the local county or extension service forestry department. But you should also check the advice on the Web sites in this chapter.

Whether you have a sick tree, or are wondering which tree to plant, the first place to head is Steve Nix's forum **Forestry from About.Com** (**http://forestry.about.com**). Steve offers regular features, a free newsletter, online chats with other tree lovers, and lots of links to tree information around the Net.

Free General Tree and Shrub Advice

Get tree-care advice at the Web site of the International Society of Arboriculture.

INTERNATIONAL SOCIETY OF ARBORICULTURE
http://www2.champaign.isa-arbor.com

"TREE SELECTION"
http://www.ag.uiuc.edu/~isa/consumer/select.html
You'll find a number of online pamphlets on tree care and selection at the home of the ISA.

THE NATIONAL ARBOR DAY FOUNDATION
http://www.arborday.org
Plant a tree with the National Arbor Day Foundation. Read tips on tree planting and care, and find out how you can purchase low-cost tree sprouts.

"TREES AND SHRUBS" FROM THE UNIVERSITY OF ILLINOIS COOPERATIVE EXTENSIVE SERVICE
http://www.ag.uiuc.edu/~robsond/solutions/horticulture/trees.html

PLANTING TREES AND SHRUBS
http://www.pbs.org/hometime/pc/lg/pc2lgpla.htm
Hometime's How-to Center provides a side-by-side comparison of and information on planting bare root, balled and burlapped, and container-grown trees and shrubs.

LANDSCAPE TREE CARE
http://www.teleport.com/~pnwisa/tree-care.html
Learn about proper tree care from the Pacific Northwest Chapter of the International Society of Aboriculture.

TREE LINK
http://www.treelink.org
Read an online version of the classic The Simple Act of Planting a Tree *and* What Tree is That, *a guide to the more common trees found in the eastern and central United States.*

ALL ABOUT TREES
http://www.amfor.org/plant/treeswhy.html
Learn where and how you should plant a tree, including how to plant for energy conservation, courtesy of American Forests.

TREE CARE TIPS & MOST FREQUENTLY ASKED QUESTIONS FROM THE NATIONAL ARBORIST ASSOCIATION
http://www.natlarb.com/tips.htm

Find answers to questions like "Why Does My Tree Look Sick?", "When Is the Best Time to Prune?", "How Do I Get Rid of Insects?", and "How Can I Protect My Trees from Storm Damage?"

TREE PLANTING GUIDE
http://www.io.com/~treefolk/guide/how.html

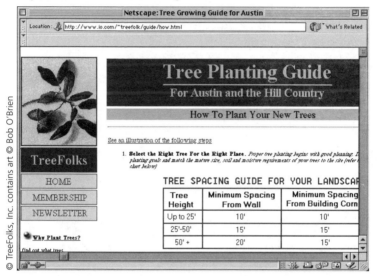

Ten guidelines for tree planting from The Tree Folks, plus links to what types of trees to plant, where to plant them, and how to care for them.

TREE AND SHRUB PLANTING GUIDELINES
http://www.ext.vt.edu/pubs/trees/430-295/430-295.html

Bonnie Lee Appleton and Susan French of the Virginia Cooperative Extension explain plant and site selection, tree and shrub preparation, and tree care after planting.

"TRANSPLANTING TREES AND SHRUBS"
BY DIANE RELF OF THE VIRGINIA COOPERATIVE EXTENSION
http://www.ext.vt.edu/departments/envirohort/articles/woody_orn amentals/transtas.html

"BRING A LITTLE SPRING INDOORS BY FORCING THE BRANCHES OF TREES AND SHRUBS"
BY JO ELLEN MEYERS SHARP
http://www.net19.com/inthegarden/articles/0298.asp

THE SIERRA CLUB
http://www.sierraclub.org

 Free Advice for Specific Types of Trees

AMERICAN CHESTNUT FOUNDATION
http://chestnut.acf.org/index.html

Learn the history of the American Chestnut and how to recognize different species in the chestnut family.

J. HILL CRADDOCK'S CHESTNUT LINKS AT CHATTANOONGA UNIVERSITY
http://www.utc.edu/~jcraddoc/chestnutlinks.html
Hundreds of links to information around the world about chestnut trees. You'll even find recipes which use chestnuts.

CHESTNUT FACT SHEETS FROM THE CONNECTICUT AGRICULTURE EXPERIMENT STATION
http://www.state.ct.us/caes/FactSheetFiles/IndexHeadingFiles/FSnut.htm

POPLARS AND WILLOWS ON THE WIDE WORLD WEB
http://poplar2.cfr.washington.edu
Learn about the history, commercial use, and scientific research on the trees known as poplar, cottonwood, aspen, and willow from Carl G. Riches and Toby Bradshaw, University of Washington.

THE BETTER HOMES & GARDENS PAW-PAW PATCH
http://www.bhglive.com/gardening
Who else but Better Homes & Gardens would create an entire Web site devoted to paw-paw love, culture, appreciation, and even recipes?

OAK WOODLAND RESOURCES
http://danr.ucop.edu/ihrmp
A collection of links to research-based information on California's hardwood rangelands, developed by the University of California.

RESTORING THE AMERICAN ELM BY THE ELM RESEARCH INSTITUTE
http://www.forelms.org
Learn how you can help return the American elm to our landscape.

Free Help Growing Bonsai

If you're thinking about trying bonsai, Allen Roffey's Bonsai Primer is a great place to start. You'll learn how to start with a blob of foliage and end up with a good-looking bonsai tree.

ALLEN'S BONSAI TREES
http://www.wmin.ac.uk/~allen

Pruning, trimming, winter protection, and what to do with a sick bonsai tree are among the many topics.

INTERNET BONSAI CLUB
http://users.nbn.net/~herrfam/Index.html

Home of the Internet Bonsai Club mailing list, this site offers online bonsai classes, an "Ask the Dr." feature where you can get help for your sick bonsai, a bonsai FAQ, and an extensive directory of suppliers, Web pages, and clubs.

BONSAI WEB
http://bonsaiweb.com

You'll find links to vendors and tools, plus a beginner's guide and a virtual tour of bonsai trees.

"BONSAI FOR BEGINNERS" BY THE UNIVERSITY OF GEORGIA COOPERATIVE EXTENSION
http://www.ces.uga.edu/cobb/bonsai.html

"GROWING BONSAI"
BY HENRY M. CATHEY, A USDA BULLETIN
http://home.maine.rr.com/michaelj/bonsai/pamphlet

THE TRUTH ABOUT AMERICAN BONSAI
http://www.esper.com/RareBird/truthbon.htm
Retired bonsai grower Charles Harnett explains how real bonsai is grown and cared for, and how to avoid imitations.

BONSAI CLUBS INTERNATIONAL
http://www.bonsai-bci.com

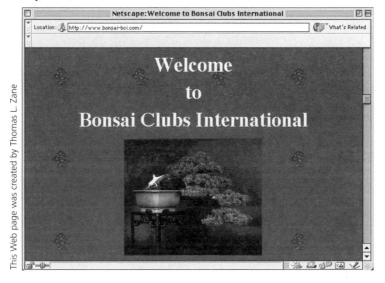

This Web page was created by Thomas L. Zane

AMERICAN BONSAI SOCIETY
http://www.absbonsai.org/abs_home.html

NATIONAL BONSAI FOUNDATION
http://www.bonsai-nbf.org

free Help Growing Flowering Shrubs

There's nothing like the perfume of a lilac bush on a sultry June evening. And what would Grandma's house be without those generations-old cascades of spirea leaves and blooms? A beautiful bush is like a giant bouquet of flowers that one can enjoy each year without investing much fuss. The Web sites in this chapter focus on care of the more persnickety shrubs like azalea and rhododendron.

For help attending to the needs of more "prosaic" shrubs like lilac, we suggest heading to the big gardening Web sites we recommend in Chapter 2. Many offer articles and discussion forums which address the problems of specific shrubs. The gardening forum on **America Online** (keyword: **garden**) is also a good source of advice.

Better Homes & Gardens' Flowering Shrubs pages (**http://www.bhglive.com/gardening/96/1-96.htm**) offer guidance with viburnum, quince, current, spirea and many other shrubs. You'll also find pruning advice.

You should also head to the **National Gardening Association**'s Web site (**http://www.garden.org**) and type the name of the shrub into its searcher. The Web site will come up with applicable articles from the archives of the NGA.

THE AMERICAN RHODODENDRON SOCIETY
http://www.rhododendron.org
Planting, pruning, and culturing are among the topics at this large site devoted to rhododendron and azalea.

THE RHODODENDRON PAGE
http://www.netaxs.com/~mckenzi1/rhodo05.html
Soil and sunlight needs, and other care requirements of rhododendron are discussed at this site, which is run by Robert J. McKenzie.

RHODODENDRON AND AZALEA NEWS
http://members.aol.com/RandANews/news.html
Betty Spady is the editor of this online publication. Learn about digging and transplanting, growing from seed, and propagation in a plastic tent. It also includes lots of links to other Web resources and an azalea exchange page.

AZALEA SOCIETY OF AMERICA
http://www.azaleas.org
The Azalea Society offers lots of information about this versatile shrub. You can join the Azalea Society or simply join their free mailing list via the link from their site.

THE INTERNATIONAL CAMELLIA SOCIETY
http://www.med-rz.uni-sb.de/med_fak/physiol2/camellia/home.htm
Learn about this exotic flowering shrub that can live up to 600 years outdoors. You'll find an extensive FAQ, resources, e-mail lists, links, and a camellia search engine.

RHODODENDRON SEASONAL CARE FROM A SANDY RHODODENDRON
http://www.rhodo.com/C-Care.cfm
You'll find help on many topics including planting, fertilizing, pruning, pinching, and watering at this nursery's Web site.

HENNING'S RHODODENDRON AND AZALEAS PAGES
http://www.users.fast.net/~shenning/rhody.html

"AZALEAS" FROM SOUTHERN LIVING ONLINE
http://southern-living.com/garden/azalea.html
What is more quintessentially southern than an azalea? Southern Living Magazine *tells you how to get southern-style blooms from your shrubs.*

THE TROPICAL HIBISCUS: QUEEN OF THE TROPICS

http://www.trop-hibiscus.com

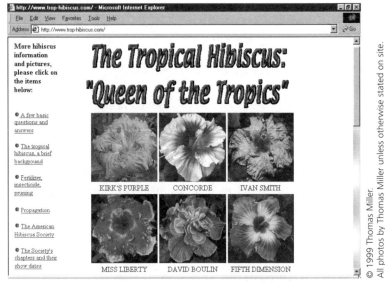

This Web site is dubbed "Happy Hibiscus for Harried Hibiscus Hopefuls (or How to Grow Tropical Hibiscus Up North)."

On this site, you will learn that there are perennial hibiscus and there are shrub-like tropical ones, some of which can grow up to 15 feet in height. You'll learn about fertilizing, pruning, and propagation. You can also join a hibiscus e-mail discussion group.

C H A P T E R   17

free Pruning Help

Disagreements over pruning have darkened marriages. There are those of us who prefer our vegetation bushy. Others insist on clipping even ragged sumacs into pleasing symmetry. Still others stamp their feet and exclaim with a scowl, "All I want is the tree to grow straight!" As long as bushes and trees flop over property lines, we'll always be bickering with spouses and neighbors over how deeply to prune the lilacs. Here are Web sites that offer sober and reasoned advice on the emotionally charged issue of pruning. For more pruning advice, articles, and Web sites head to Deborah Simpson's pruning page on **About.Com**'s Garden site (**http://gardening.about.com**).

"HOW TO PRUNE TREES" BY THE UNITED STATES DEPARTMENT OF AGRICULTURE, FOREST SERVICE
http://willow.ncfes.umn.edu/HT_prune/prun001.htm
This the official word. Take it for what it's worth.

"PRUNING ORNAMENTAL SHRUBS" FROM THE UNIVERSITY OF MISSOURI–COLUMBIA
http://muextension.missouri.edu/xplor/agguides/hort/g06870.htm
You can either read this guide—or listen to it. We promise it's better than listening to a spouse cry "Don't cut that branch!"

PRUNING GUIDELINES FROM THE MINISTRY OF FOREST, VICTORIA, BRITISH COLUMBIA
http://www.for.gov.bc.ca/tasb/legsregs/fpc/fpcguide/pruning/pruntoc.htm

PRUNING TREES AND SHRUBS
http://www.pbs.org/hometime/pc/lg/pc2lgprn.htm
From PBS's Hometime's How-to Center comes a guide to pruning mature trees and young ones, shrubs, renewal pruning, and pruning formal hedges.

PRUNING TIPS FOR HEALTHIER PLANTS
http://www.fiskars.com/gardeners/pruning_tips/prune.html
Learn when and how to prune, from sheers-maker Fiskars.

"GUIDELINES TO CORRECT PRUNING," BY DR. ALEX SHIGO
http://www.teleport.com/~pnwisa/shigo.html

"GUIDE TO SUCCESSFUL PRUNING" BY SUSAN C. FRENCH & BONNIE LEE APPLETON, VIRGINIA COOPERATIVE EXTENSION.
http://www.ext.vt.edu/pubs/trees/430-455/430-455.html

BASIC PRINCIPLES OF PRUNING WOODY PLANTS
http://www.ces.uga.edu/pubcd/b949-w.html
G.L. Wade and Robert R. Westerfield from The University of Georgia College of Agricultural & Environmental Sciences Cooperative Extension Service explain the principles through illustrations.

 **Help for Landscaping & Garden Design**

The hardest part of turning a ho-hum backyard into a charming nature getaway is deciding how to landscape it. Should you plant a spruce in front of the telephone pole? Would a fountain look good under the birch? Should you use lannon stone or boulders to carve a walkway through the trees? And where, oh where, will the rose trellis fit? These are difficult decisions. If you make them carelessly you run the risk of turning your yard into a higgledy-piggledy mess.

The first place to head on the Web for landscaping help is **Mary Anne Lynch's Landscaping Forum at About.Com** (**http://landscaping.about.com/home/garden/landscaping/mbody.htm** or **http://landscaping.about.com**). Mary Anne offers an outstanding selection of articles, tips and how-tos on everything from planning decks and stone walks to selecting trees. She also offers links to all the very best Web resources that will help in your landscaping decisions.

Make landscaping decisions more confidently by tapping into About.Com's landscaping forum.

"LANDSCAPING YOUR FRONT YARD"
http://muextension.missouri.edu/xplor/agguides/hort/g06905.htm
Learn how to graph out and design your landscaping master plan taking into account the architectural features of your house, the entranceways, the trees and shrubs you want to highlight, and other concerns.

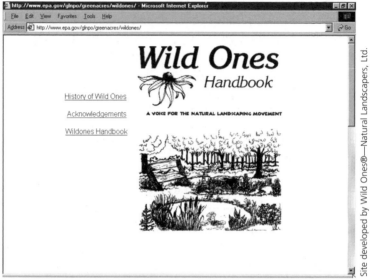

Site developed by Wild Ones®—Natural Landscapers, Ltd.

Want to "naturally landscape" your yard but worried about irritating the neighbors? The Wild Ones suggests creating a boundary between your yard and the neighbors' through hedges or fences, and adding elements such as stone paths that suggest that the yard is not simply overgrown.

THE WILD ONES HANDBOOK
http://www.epa.gov/glnpo/greenacres/wildones
The Wild Ones is a non-profit club of natural landscapers that promote the concept of planting native plants instead of lawns, as well as other "natural" landscaping techniques. Their complete guidebook is online, courtesy of the Environmental Protection Agency, and it's full of great ideas.

Plan Your Landscape Virtually with Landscape Design Software

It's sometimes hard to visualize what a conifer spruce will look like in ten years. It's even harder to imagine what a raised garden mound or retaining wall will look like once it's built. Landscape design software lets you "see" what your garden plans will look like five, ten or twenty years from now. Good design packages come with hundreds of pre-drawn shrubs and trees that you can view in three dimensions on your computer screen as you place them in a layout of your yard, then watch them age. You can download free demos of the programs from some of these Web sites.

ABRACADATA'S DESIGN YOUR OWN HOME LANDSCAPE FROM ABRACADATA
http://www.abracadata.com/land.html
(Windows, DOS, Macintosh)

LANDDESIGNER
http://www.sierra.com/sierrahome/gardening/titles/cld
(Windows)

LANDSCAPE
http://www.ili.net/~knight/land1.html
(Windows)
Software for managing a landscaping company.

Estimate What You Need for Your Landscape With Free Calculator Sierra offers an online calculator (**http://www.sierra.com/sierrahome/gardening/calculators**) that will tabulate your project costs on a per cubic yard basis.

DESIGN PRINCIPLES IN GARDEN-MAKING, BY LINDA ENGSTROM
http://www.teleport.com/~lengstro/DESIGN.htm

Linda Engstrom, a landscape designer, shares some of her tips for creating a special place in your yard.

THE CREATIVE GARDENER—ADVENTURES IN ARTISTIC GARDEN MAKING
http://guitarweb.music.duq.edu/lpurse/welcome.html

Lynn Purse's unique site focuses on the use of color and design to plan unique gardens.

WILDLAND WEEDS MANAGEMENT & RESEARCH FROM THE NATURE CONSERVANCY
http://tncweeds.ucdavis.edu

*Find out how to control the weeds that destroy natural habitats. Be sure to visit **The Nature Conservancy**'s main Web site (**http://www.tnc.org**) for more links and information on helping to sustain the natural environment.*

"DEVELOPING THE LANDSCAPING PLAN" BY UNIVERSITY OF MISSOURI–COLUMBIA EXTENSION
http://muextension.missouri.edu/xplor/agguides/hort/g06901.htm

HTGROVER—
LANDSCAPE PLANT SELECTION KNOWLEDGEBASE
http://www.clr.toronto.edu:1080/cgi-bin/GROVER/htgrover?fields

Enter your plain type, USDA zone, size, and other criteria to select plants for your landscape design, courtesy of the University of Toronto.

FREE PLANTS
http://www.freeplants.com

Mike McGroarty explains in detail everything you can imagine about propagating all kinds of landscape plants. Mike also offers pruning tips and explains how to use ground cover for weed control, how to keep deer and rabbits from ruining your trees and shrubs, and much more.

Free Help Designing a Japanese or Chinese Garden

JAPANESE GARDEN DATABASE
http://pobox.upenn.edu/~cheetham/jgarden/index.html

Beautiful examples of garden art, plus reference materials and links to many Web resources.

ICONOGRAPHY OF CHINESE GARDENS
http://www.intranet.csupomona.edu/~ige/gardens/1h1.htm

JAPANESE GARDEN
http://mcel.pacificu.edu/as/students/chee/garden.html

JAPANESE GARDENING
http://plaza.people.or.jp/garden/en

 ## JAPANESE GARDENS FORUM ON GARDEN WEB
http://www.gardenweb.com/forums/jgard

CHINA, MOTHER OF ALL GARDENS
http://www.china-gardens.com
You'll find lots of information on creating Chinese gardens, selecting flowers and plants, and landscaping.

THE CLASSICAL CHINESE GARDEN SOCIETY
http://www.chinesegarden.org
Learn how this society is building a Suzhou-style urban garden in Portland, Oregon. The Web site includes photos and links to Web resources that will help you build your own garden.

CHAPTER 19

Help Attracting Birds, Butterflies, and Other Wildlife to Your Yard

What's a garden without butterflies? And what gardener doesn't feel a thrill of success when hummingbirds come to feast on the nectar of his or her flowers? For many, gardening and attracting birds and wildlife are inseparable passions. You can make your yard more popular with local wildlife by merely adding a few special bushes and planting the sorts of flowers that winged creatures crave. Start by heading to **Deb & Chris's Bird and Butterfly Plant List at About.Com (http://gardening.about.com/home/garden/gardening/library/weekly/aa052798.htm)**. About.Com gardening guide **Deb Simpson (http://gardening.about.com)** has put together an ambitious database of plants chosen for nectar, seeds, berries, cover or windbreak. You'll find information on the plants' required growing conditions and USDA zones, along with links to Web sites and references on the plants.

BACKYARD BIRDING
http://www.bcpl.net/~tross/by/backyard.html
Terry Ross hosts a wonderful site with links to government pamphlets and information on growing habitats for different types of birds and wildlife. He also offers lots of backyard birding information, including recipes, ideas on landscaping to attract birds, and directions on how to build birdhouses.

BIRD YARD BY TOR IVAR BJØNNESS
http://home.sol.no/~tibjonn/birdyard.htm
Although this Web site is in Norway, it's one of the top "backyard bird" sites on the Net because of its extensive information on attracting all types of birds to your yard. It also features information on joining mailing list discussion groups for backyard bird lovers.

"PLANTS WHICH ATTRACT HUMMINGBIRDS" BY AMBER HEARN
http://www.anet-chi.com/~manytimes/amber/humflws.htm

**"BACKYARD WILDLIFE TIPS FOR SUCCESS"
FROM THE UNIVERSITY OF NEBRASKA
COOPERATIVE EXTENSION**
http://www.ianr.unl.edu/pubs/Wildlife/g1332.HTM

**"CREATE A WILDLIFE GARDEN"
FROM *ORGANIC GARDENING MAGAZINE***
http://www.organicgardening.com/articles/article2.html

**"PLANTING FOR HABITATS" FROM THE UNIVERSITY
OF NEBRASKA COOPERATIVE EXTENSION**
http://www.ianr.unl.edu/pubs/Wildlife/g671.htm

**"PLANTING FOR HUMMINGBIRDS & BUTTERFLIES"
FROM NORTH CAROLINA STATE UNIVERSITY
EXTENSION**
http://www.ces.ncsu.edu/nreos/forest/steward/www20.html

**"SHRUBS FOR WILDLIFE" FROM THE NEBRASKA
GAME & PARKS COMMISSION**
http://www.ngpc.state.ne.us/wildlife/shrubs.html

© Joyce T. Schillen 1996

*Joyce Schillen offers essays on attracting butterflies to your garden at
The Garden Pages (**http://www.gardenpages.com**).*

free Help Building Ponds & Growing Aquatic Gardens

There's something magical about a pond. The gracefully float-ing waterlilies and the goldfish skittering below bestow a sense of serenity and wonder that no other kind of garden can match. Like most gardeners, you have probably toyed with the idea of digging a pond, but worried that you'll end up with an unsightly hole full of stagnant water. The Web pages in this chapter offer inspiration, direction, and even building plans for ponds. And if you don't have a quarter-acre to bulldoze, fear not; there's even a Web site that will show you how to cultivate a water garden in a whiskey barrel! So gather your koi and pass out the buckets. It's pond building time!

Free Pond Building Help

"BUILDING A POND" BY GUY LOVREN
http://www.exit109.com/~gosta/pond.sht
Guy has written an online book complete with illustrations. He offers no-nonsense advice on pond building, installing a filtration pump, creating waterfalls, and more.

"THE VERY SMALL POND OR THE VERY LARGE PUDDLE" BY JOHN ROGERS
http://wkweb4.cableinet.co.uk/JohnRogers/pond.htm
John details his pond-building experiences. Use the Web site to figure out if you have the room to build a pond, where it should be built, if it should have running water, and more. John also offers a Java applet for calculating pond water volume.

BRAD'S FREE WATER GARDENING ADVICE
http://members.aol.com/Shubun/index.html
Brad, who lives in Chicago, details a nifty way to start water gardening—putting your garden in an inexpensive whiskey barrel. He offers info on filtration and skimmers.

HALF BARREL POND PAGE
http://www.jeffcook.com/hbpond.html
Jeffrey Valjean Cook explains the basics of building a barrel pond and lists resources and mail-order suppliers.

 ## More Free Pond Help

From the Usenet newsgroup **rec.ponds** comes this extensive collection of the most frequently asked questions, from lining ponds to determining pond depth.

To read the messages in rec.ponds, *check out instructions in Chapter 1 for signing up for newsgroups.*

POND CONSTRUCTION FAQ
http://w3.one.net/~rzutt/genfaq.html

POND MAINTENANCE FAQ
http://w3.one.net/~rzutt/maintenance.html

ORGANIC PONDKEEPING FAQ
http://w3.one.net/~rzutt/organic.html

POND PLANTS FAQ
http://w3.one.net/~rzutt/plant.html

PETE'S POND PAGE
http://reality.sgi.com/peteo
Pete Orelup shares photos of his gorgeous pond, its water plants, and the surrounding gardens. He gives information on its biological filtration system, its waterfall, and more.

Interested in Hydroponics?
Check Out These Sites:

🛒 INTER URBAN WATER FARMS ONLINE
http://www.viasub.net/IUWF/index.html

HYDROPONICS B.C.
http://www.hydroponicsbc.com/hydroponics.html

HOMEGROWN HYDROPONICS
http://www.hydroponics.com

INTRODUCTION TO HYDROPONICS
http://www.cropking.com/cropking/intro

 **🛒 THE POND PAGES**
http://www.thepondpages.com
You'll find help on installing your pond and instructions on how to calculate the volume of your pond. Visit the discussion boards to post your questions.

GREG'S POND AND KOI FARM
http://soli.inav.net/~bickal/pond.htm

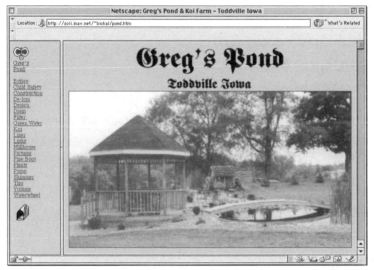

Learn all about Greg's pond, including how he constructed it, his drain and filtering system, how he cleared his green water, and more, at this fascinating site.

VICTORIA WATERLILY WEB PAGE
http://www.h2olily.com/vic.html
Victoria waterlilies are huge waterlilies from South America, but many people grow them in large ponds. Read how. There's also a live Victoria-cam!

NORTH TEXAS WATER GARDEN SOCIETY
http://www.ntwgs.org

NORTHERN POND
http://www.northernpond.com
Click the Journal link for an index of interesting photo essays on gardening and ponds.

![leaf icon] Magazines About Ponds

THE INTERNET PONDER
http://www.viagrafix.net/pingle/ip99/index.html
The online magazine of the Internet Pond Society.

WATERGARDEN MAGAZINE
http://www.watergardening.com
Subscription information, photos, some tips, and links.

Free Advice on Koi

PAUL'S KOI PAGE
http://www.koi.uk.com

© 1997 Paul James

What's a water garden without koi? Paul James shares photos of his pond, details its construction, and explains his filtration systems.

You'll find information on the varieties of koi and plenty of helpful links. If that's not enough, download the free koi wallpaper for your computer.

KOI NET
http://www.vcnet.com/koi_net
A guide to Koi and Koi ponds

 **🛒 *Are Your Koi Not Feeling Well?*** Visit Dr. Erik Johnson, the Koi Vet (**http://www.koivet.com/index.html**) for information on Koi diseases, medicines, resources, and everything you need to know for keeping your pond denizens healthy.

 Want to See More Personal Pond Pages? Visit the Internet Pond Society (**http://w3.one.net/~rzutt/index.html**) and its personal pond page list (**http://w3.one.net/~rzutt/alink.html#personal**).

free Help Tackling the Peccadilloes of Your Climate

Move your garden forty miles in any direction and, as our mothers would say, it's like cooking on a different stove. Everything ripens and blooms at a different pace. You need to start your pumpkins earlier and plant your peas later. The blue-bells that bloomed in profusion on your old homestead may wither in a slightly more arid home. But it's not only climate that determines how lush your hyacinths and how green your valley. Local soils are also responsible. A Georgia peach wouldn't be a Georgia peach without that Georgia clay. And we know people who swear that certain herbs pack more zing when grown in the glacial soils around the Great Lakes.

Whether you and your plants live nomadic or rooted (ahem) lives, you'll love the Web sites in this chapter. They offer advice for gardening in specific locales. There are Web sites that tell you how to get your impatiens through South Florida winters without them losing their flowers. There are Web sites that tell you when to apply nitrogen to pecan trees grown in the low desert. There are even Web sites devoted to urban gardening.

Find Gardening Schedules and Tips for Your Region

To find gardening advice specific to your locale head to **The Virtual Garden** (**http://www.vg.com**) and click Regional Gardener. You can determine your growing zone, find the zone's frost date, and tap into a planting schedule for your zone, as well as get gardening tips.

Let the Virtual Garden help you determine your growing zone and frost date.

You should also tap into the Web site of your local extension office. You'll find addresses for the Web sites of the major extension Web sites in Chapter 22. To find the Web site of your local extension office tap into **Gardenscape** (**http://www.gardenscape.com/GSEducation.html**). Or visit the Web site of **Texas A&M**'s horticulture program for a list (**http://aggie-horticulture.tamu.edu/introhtml/univers.html**).

Web Sites About Gardening in the Northeast

BOSTON GARDENING
http://www.bostongardens.com/index.cfm

Tap into Boston Gardening for news, articles, and tips on gardening in the Boston area.

ROCHESTER (NY) GARDENING
http://www.rochestergardening.com

Web Sites About Gardening in the Mid-Atlantic Region

Visit Metro New York Home & Garden for news and forums about gardening in the city.

METRO NEW YORK HOME & GARDEN
http://www.nygardener.com

A large collection of resources for gardeners in New York, New Jersey, and Connecticut.

GREEN GUERILLAS
http://www.users.interport.net/~ggsnyc/index.html

Green Guerillas is a New York organization that transforms abandoned lots and rooftops into community gardens.

THE MID-ATLANTIC REGIONAL FRUIT LOOP
http://www.caf.wvu.edu/Kearneysville/fruitloop.html
Several universities, including Virginia Tech, West Virginia University, the University of Maryland, Penn State, and Rutgers provide information on deciduous fruit trees.

ASSATEAGUE PLANTS OF THE THICKET AND MARITIME FOREST AREAS
http://www.assateague.com/pl-thick.html
Photos and descriptions of plants of the maritime forest from the Chesapeake barrier island.

 *Web Sites About Gardening in the Southeast*

ATLANTA GARDENING
http://www.atlgarden.com
A wonderful collection of garden resources for Georgia and metropolitan Atlanta.

CAROLINA GARDENER
http://www.carolinagardener.com
Read features from the Southeast's leading magazine for gardeners.

GARDENING IN NORTH CAROLINA
http://www.ces.ncsu.edu/depts/hort/consumer
Sponsored by the North Carolina Cooperative Extension Service.

"FLOWERING PERENNIALS FOR GEORGIA GARDENS" BY PAUL THOMAS, THE UNIVERSITY OF GEORGIA COLLEGE COOPERATIVE EXTENSION SERVICE
http://www.ces.uga.edu/pubcd/b944-w.html

⚡ Web Sites About Gardening in the South

SOUTHERN LIVING GARDENS
http://www.southernliving.com/garden/index.html
Visit the Web site of Southern Living *magazine for lots of gardening advice, tips, and articles.*

"FLOWERING PERENNIALS FOR GEORGIA GARDENS" FROM THE UNIVERSITY OF GEORGIA COOPERATIVE EXTENSION
http://www.ces.uga.edu/pubcd/b944-w.html

"FLOWERING BULBS FOR GEORGIA GARDENS"
http://www.ces.uga.edu/pubcd/b918-w.html

SOUTHERN GARDENING
http://www.southerngardening.com

Terrific information about gardening in the coastal South, from the Texas Gulf coast to the Atlantic coast of South Carolina.

Web Sites About Gardening on the Gulf Coast

HIGHER GROUND:
THE LIFE AND TIMES OF A SOUTHERN GARDEN
http://www.flash.net/~elang/index.htm

This site promotes perennial and mixed border designs suited to Gulf Coast gardens.

ORNAMENTAL HORTICULTURE FOR THE HOUSTON AND GULF COAST AREA
http://www.ghg.net/beyer/hortpage.htm

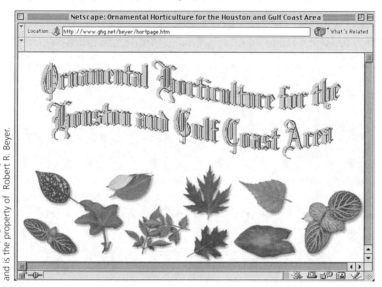

This web page was created by and is the property of Robert R. Beyer.

Bob and Lana Byer share ornamental horticulture information and links for gardeners in the Houston and Gulf Coast area.

MONTH BY MONTH LANDSCAPE GUIDE FOR TROPICAL SOUTH FLORIDA
http://mgonline.com/monthly.html

From Master Gardener Landscaping of Fort Lauderdale.

🛒 **FLORIDA PLANTS ONLINE**
http://www.floridaplants.com

 FLORIDATA
http://www.floridata.com

Hundreds of plant profiles with descriptions, growing instructions, and photographs. Many from Florida scrub natural plant communities. New articles added monthly.

Web Sites About Gardening in the Mountains

GARDENING IN THE ROCKIES
http://www.colostate.edu/Depts/CoopExt/PUBS/COLUMNGW/gwmenu.html

Colorado State Cooperative Extension provides weekly gardening tips and articles.

ORGANIC GARDENING'S ALMANAC
http://www.organicgardening.com/almanac/

Follow the link to monthly gardening tips for the conditions in your hardiness zone.

Web Sites About Gardening in the Midwest

THE (NO) PROBLEM GARDEN
http://www.netusa1.net/~lindley

Lindley Karstens says that just as there are no bad dogs, there are no bad gardens. This Web site is about natural gardening in the Midwest and how to get the most attractive green and flowering stuff with the least amount of time, effort, and money.

THE WISCONSIN GARDENER
http://www.wpt.org/garden/index.html

Articles and other resources for Wisconsin gardeners from the Wisconsin Public Television show Wisconsin Gardener.

GARDENING IN ILLINOIS
http://garden-gate.prairienet.org/gardill.htm

For gardeners in east central Illinois, Karen Fletcher has compiled information, organizations, and interesting places to visit.

METRO ST. LOUIS GARDENER'S GUIDE
http://www.stlgarden.com

Sections on garden design, roses, perennials, and lawns are featured. You can also subscribe to "The Latest Dirt," a free monthly newsletter.

WEEKLY GARDENING NEWS FOR CENTRAL OHIO
http://www.hcs.ohio-state.edu/wgn.html

For central Ohio gardening challenges, this site (from the Ohio State University Extension) is updated weekly between April and October.

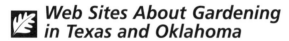

Web Sites About Gardening in the Southwest

THE DESERT GARDENER
http://www.azstarnet.com/~bmitton
A nifty online magazine for gardeners in the Tucson area.

MARY BERTH VENDER-FAY'S ARIZONA GARDENING HOMEPAGE
http://www.goodnet.com/~eb43571/garden.html
For gardeners in the desert Southwest, this site offers hints and resources, including information on public gardens, organizations, and commercial suppliers.

TIMELY TIPS FOR GARDENING IN THE LOW DESERT
http://ag.arizona.edu/maricopa/garden/html/t-tips/t-tips.htm
Select a month and Timely Tips will tell you the typical rainfall and temperature patterns, as well as what to do in the garden. FAQs from the University of Arizona Cooperative Extension.

Web Sites About Gardening in Texas and Oklahoma

THE AUSTIN GARDEN FAQ
http://www.paisano.com/gardens/gardening.html
Rusty Mase maintains this Web site as a place for Austin gardeners to share tips and hints.

 **Web Sites About Gardening in the Northwest**

PACIFIC NORTHWEST GARDENING
http://www.nwgardening.com

Learn why gardening in the Pacific Northwest is different from gardening in any other part of the country.

SLUGS AND SALALS:
GARDENING IN THE PACIFIC NORTHWEST
http://www.slugsandsalal.com

Weekly articles, tips, community happenings, and more about gardening in Washington State, British Columbia, and Oregon.

TWO RAINY SIDE GARDENERS
http://www.rainyside.com

Debra Teachout-Teashon and Travis Saling run this site for gardeners in the maritime Pacific Northwest region.

VEGETABLE GARDENS OF THE COLUMBIA BASIN
http://www.poplaracre.com

You'll read practical vegetable gardening advice for the Columbia Basin region of southeast Washington and northeast Oregon.

Web Sites About Gardening in California

GARDENING IN CENTRAL CALIFORNIA
http://www.elite.net/~tjohnson/garden.htm
Teman Johnson share hints and links to other Web resources.

THE BAY AREA GARDENER
http://www.gardens.com
An extensive resource for gardeners in the San Francisco Bay area.

MASTER GARDENERS OF THE SANTA CLARA COUNTY—GARDENING TIPS
http://www.mastergardeners.org/tips/tips.html
An index of gardening tips sorted by month.

DIGITALSEED—A SOUTHERN CALIFORNIA GARDENING RESOURCE
http://www.digitalseed.com/index.html
Digitalseed offers plenty of gardening information tailored to the Southern California gardener, including a directory of local gardening resources, an online forum, and lots of practical advice.

Web Sites About Gardening Abroad

Here is a selection of Web sites for gardeners abroad. For more links, visit the big gardening sites we recommend in Chapter 2.

EAST COAST CANADIAN GARDENER
http://www.klis.com/fundy/ecg/home.htm

GARDENS OF THE GOLDEN HORSESHOE (SOUTHEASTERN ONTARIO)
http://www.interlog.com/~ggh/ggh.htm

Check Gardening Weather with The Weather Channel. You can check the gardening weather in your neighborhood with the **Weather Channel's** home and garden maps (**http://www.weather.com/gardening**). You'll find maps of morning and afternoon forecasts, as well as long-range forecasts.

THE GARDEN CLUB: IRELAND'S ONLINE GARDENING RESOURCE
http://www.clubi.ie/garden-club/index.html

MEDITERRANEAN CLIMATE GARDENING THROUGHOUT THE WORLD
http://www.support.net/medit-plants

GARDEN WORLD—UK GARDEN CENTERS
http://www.gardenworld.co.uk/garden_main.html

SOCIETY FOR GROWING AUSTRALIAN PLANTS
http://www.iweb.net.au/~sgap

GARDENS SOUTH (SOUTH AFRICA)
http://www.pix.za/garden

NEW ZEALAND GARDENS ONLINE
http://www.gardens.co.nz

GARDENING PAGES FOR NEW ZEALAND
http://www.manawatu.gen.nz/~garden

 **Gardening Advice from Extension Services**

Working in conjunction with the U.S. Dept. of Agriculture, university extension services have provided invaluable information to generations of gardeners and farmers. Tap into their Web sites to read the plant fact sheets and pamphlets that you used to need to mail away for. In many chapters of this book we've listed university extension Web sites that we think are useful, but this chapter lists the main directories of some of the largest extension sites. If you're looking for an extension service in your area, head to the Web site of **The Cooperative State, Research, Education, and Extension Service of the USDA (http://www.reeusda.gov)**. Click "State Partners" **(http://www.reeusda.gov/1700/statepartners/usa.htm)** for a directory of state agencies.

UNIVERSITY OF ILLINOIS EXTENSION—HORTICULTURE AND HOME GARDEN
http://www.extension.uiuc.edu/home/homelawn.html
Among the library of information here you'll find:

HOME YARD AND GARDEN PEST
http://www.ag.uiuc.edu/cespubs/hyg

HORT CORNER
http://www.urbanext.uiuc.edu/hort/index.html

HORTICULTURAL SOLUTION SERIES
http://www.ag.uiuc.edu/~robsond/solutions/solutions.html

PEST MANAGEMENT AND CROP DEVELOPMENT
http://www.ag.uiuc.edu/cespubs/pest

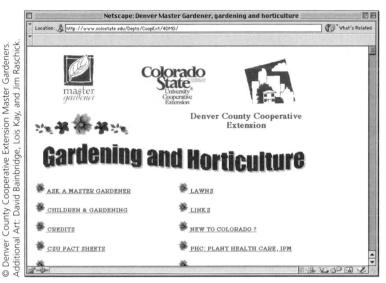

A master gardener is just an e-mail away, waiting to answer your gardening questions on the Colorado State University Colorado Extension Web site.

DENVER COUNTY COOPERATIVE EXTENSION GARDENING & HORTICULTURE
http://www.colostate.edu/Depts/CoopExt/4DMG
You'll find lots of gardening information here on flowers, fruits and vegetables, soil, trees, and shrubs.

OHIO STATE WEB GARDEN
http://www.hcs.ohio-state.edu/webgarden.html

PLANT DICTIONARY
http://www.hcs.ohio-state.edu/plants.html

FACTSHEET DATABASE
http://www.hcs.ohio-state.edu/factsheet.html

LANDSCAPE AND NURSERY DIALOG
http://www.hcs.ohio-state.edu/hcs/webgarden/Land/Land.html

UNIVERSITY OF MINNESOTA EXTENSION SERVICE
http://www.extension.umn.edu/Documents/titles.html?supercat=D&cat=G

Over 160 documents on many topics including "Accessible Gardening for Therapeutic Horticulture" and "You Can Be a Master Gardener."

PURDUE'S VIRTUAL PLANT & PEST DIAGNOSTIC LABORATORY
http://www.ppdl.purdue.edu/ppdl

Diagnose your plant's pests at Purdue's virtual pest diagnostic lab.

PURDUE UNIVERSITY CONSUMER HORTICULTURE PAGE
http://www.hort.purdue.edu/ext/ConHort.html

PURDUE GARDENING NEWS ARTICLES
http://www.hort.purdue.edu/ext/news_stories.html

PURDUE'S DOWN THE GARDEN PATH NEWSLETTER
http://www.ppdl.purdue.edu/ppdl/Newsletters.html#DGP

Published 17 times per year, available as a free download.

CORNELL'S FLORACULTURE & ORNAMENTAL HORTICULTURE
http://www.cals.cornell.edu/dept/flori

ORNAMENTAL LANDSCAPE FROM DELAWARE COOPERATIVE EXTENSION
http://bluehen.ags.udel.edu/deces/orn-land/orn-list.htm

HORTICULTURE AND HOME PEST NEWS FROM IOWA STATE UNIVERSITY EXTENSION
http://www.ipm.iastate.edu/ipm/hortnews
You'll find resources on general horticulture, house plants, insects, outdoor plants, plant diseases, small fruits, trees and shrubs, tree fruits, and grass.

HORTICULTURE FROM NEBRASKA COOPERATIVE EXTENSION
http://www.ianr.unl.edu/pubs/Horticulture/

HAWAII COOPERATIVE EXTENSION SERVICE
http://agrss.sherman.hawaii.edu/hort/digest/index.html

VIRGINIA COOPERATIVE EXTENSION CONSUMER HORTICULTURE
http://www.ext.vt.edu:4040/eis/owa/docdb.getcat?cat=ir-ln
The site offers a fact sheet covering landscape and nursery topics.

HOME HORTICULTURE—MICHIGAN STATE UNIVERSITY EXTENSION
http://www.msue.msu.edu/msue/imp/mod03/master03.html
Tap into 1,800 plant fact sheets in an alphabetical database covering everything from Aaronsbeard St. John's Wort to a Zygocactus.

YARD & GARDEN FROM NEW MEXICO COOPERATIVE EXTENSION
http://www.cahe.nmsu.edu/ces/yard

Curtis W. Smith writes a weekly column on garden and landscape care problems. You can search through an archive of past articles.

Search the files of the New Mexico Cooperative Extension for answers to your southwestern plant and pest problems.

By the way, you don't have to live in the United States to benefit from visiting these Web sites. Tap into an extension service in a climate similar to yours for relevant growing advice.

free Help Growing Orchids

Don't listen to Joan Rivers when she says that nothing ages one like an orchid corsage. If Judy and Gloria had their way we'd all be wearing orchids tucked in our bosoms every day. Maybe you're the more understated sort who prefers to keep an orchid blooming in a pot on the kitchen sink. Or maybe you've succumbed to orchid mania and have transformed a spare bedroom or two with trees full of exotic blooms. Did you know that there are over 20,000 varieties of orchids? To some that means "too many species, too little time." That's why it's important to get the orchid growing advice you need fast. To that end, the best place to quickly appease your orchid mania is **Orchids on the WWW http://www.chebucto.ns.ca/Recreation/OrchidSNS/wwwsites.html**. Hosted by the Canadian Orchid Congress and the Orchid Society of Nova Scotia, Orchids on the WWW offers links to orchid Web sites and information around the world, plus links to botanical gardens and conservatories that feature orchids.

More Big Orchid Web Sites that Offer Orchid Lovers Help (Psychological and Otherwise)

THE AMERICAN ORCHID SOCIETY'S ORCHID WEB
http://orchidweb.org

If you're just starting to grow orchids, this is a great site to visit, since it offers lots of advice for beginners, including help on buying orchids and growing them on trees. The site even offers a pronunciation guide to orchid names so you don't feel like a complete fool at the first orchid convention you attend.

THE ORCHID HOUSE

http://retirees.uwaterloo.ca:80/~jerry/orchids

Netscape: The Orchid House
Location: http://retirees.uwaterloo.ca:80/~jerry/orchids/
What's Related
Brassocattleya Setting Sun
The Orchid House
In the world of flowers, orchids are the undisputed champions. Once the expensive interest of the wealthy, orchids today are within reach of all. One of the oldest and best organized of plant hobbies, orchid culture now enjoys worldwide popularity. Their

This Web site created by Jerome Bolce.

Jerry Bolce offers a guide to artificial lighting, information on plant nutrition, a FAQ with basic orchid culturing advice, and links to other Web resources on orchids.

THE ORCHID RESOURCE

http://www.botana.com/tors.html

Bruce Ide, Sr. hosts this guide to orchid history and the rules of orchid culture.

TIP

Send an Orchid E-mail Postcard to a Pal! Head to iCards (**http://students.washington.edu/dhwang/icards**) to send an orchid card to a friend. Select a photo, add some music, compose your message, and send it to your friend's e-mail address.

🛒 PHALS.COM: ONLINE ORCHID CARE AND BASIC CULTURE GUIDE
http://www.phals.com

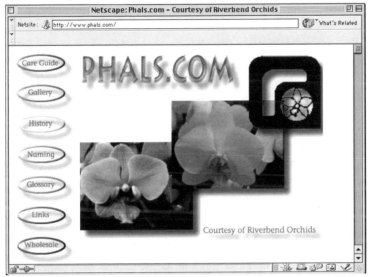

Riverbend Orchids offers an orchid care guide, a gallery, a history of orchids, and a glossary.

More Free Orchid Growing Advice

ORCHID FAQ VERSION 1.4
http://vengers.com/faq/faq14toc.htm
Aaron J. Hicks has compiled extensive information on how to grow orchids, solve orchid problems, and even grow orchids on your office windowsill.

ORCHID GROWING FOR THE HORTICULTURALLY CHALLENGED
http://www.shreve.net/~marylois/pageone.html
Craig Reavis has been growing orchids for over twenty years and has put together a marvelous primer on how anyone can start growing orchids in their home.

THE AMAZING WORLD OF ORCHIDS
http://www.shreve.net/~rainforest

Lois Greer shares pictures and explanations of orchids ranging from the diminutive to the weird.

THE ORCHID WEBLOPEDIA
http://conbio.bio.uci.edu/orchid

Reference databases on orchids, and a very active bulletin board for orchid lovers to post questions.

THE ORCHID PHOTO PAGE
http://www.orchidworks.com

Looking for tips on photographing orchids? Read Greg Allikas' advice, and view a gallery of over 200 of Greg's photos. Be sure to take a look at his virtual orchid hybrid demonstration, called "What if They Mated?"

FRAGRANT ORCHID SPECIES
http://www.chebucto.ns.ca/Recreation/OrchidSNS/frag.html

Sydney H. Yearron, a member of the Victoria (British Columbia) Orchid Society, offers an alphabetized list of orchid species with their type, strength, and time of fragrance.

PLANT VIRUSES—KNOWN SUSCEPTIBILITIES OF ORCHIDACEAE
http://biology.anu.edu.au/Groups/MES/vide/famly094.htm

Descriptions from the Virus Identification Data Exchange database.

 🛒 ***Shopping for Orchids?*** Visit Orchid Mania's World's Best Commercial Orchid Grower's Page (**http://www.orchids.org/growers.html**) for links to Web sites of orchid nurseries around the world. **The Orchid Mall** (**http://www.orchidmall.com**) offers supplies. OrchidLink.Com (**http://www.orchidlink.com/grower.htm**) offers a directory of orchid growers organized by state and country.

A DIFFERENT WAY TO GROW ORCHIDS— HID LIGHTING
http://quickval.com/hid.htm
Kenneth M. Rossman explains how to grow orchids using high intensity-discharge lighting.

HORTICULTURAL EXHIBITIONS: DISCOVER ORCHIDS
http://www.si.edu/resource/tours/gardens/orchids/start.htm
Learn how to propagate orchids from seeds, find out how orchids are pollinated, and see pictures of the exhibit presented by the Smithsonian Institution and the United States Botanic Garden.

🛒 PHALAENOPSIS.NET
http://www.phalaenopsis.net

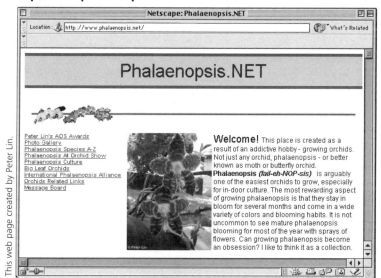

Peter Lin shares photos and information on the phalaenopsis, also called the "moth" or "butterfly" orchid—one of the easiest orchids to grow.

ABBREVIATIONS USED IN ORCHID CULTURES
http://www.txdirect.net/users/chrisort/abb.htm

Web Sites of Orchid Lovers' Magazines

ORCHID DIGEST QUARTERLY PUBLICATION
http://www.shreve.net/~orchidigest
Read articles from this magazine for orchid fans.

ORCHIDS AUSTRALIA
http://www.infoweb.com.au:80/orchids/index.htm
The official publication of the Australian Council, Inc. and Australia's leading orchid magazine.

 ## Orchid Mailing Lists and Forums

THE ORCHID GUIDE DIGEST
http://www.orchidguide.com
Orchid Guide Digest is an e-mail based discussion group of hundreds of orchid lovers the world over hosted by Kenneth Bruyninckx. To sign up e-mail majordomo@orchidguide.com. In the message, type: subscribe orchids-digest youremailaddress, as in subscribe orchids-digest janesmith@myisp.com.

THE ORCHID LIST DIGEST ARCHIVES
http://129.93.226.138/orchid/orchid.htm
You can read messages posted in the past to the old Orchid List Digest mailing list.

Travel The Orchid Web Ring to Visit the Web Pages of Orchid Lovers
Surf the Web pages of orchid fanatics around the world by tapping into the **Orchid Web Ring** (**http://www.orchidsasia.com/orcring.htm**). This page is a starting point for visiting interlinked orchid sites. It also offers a beginner's guide to orchids.

Planning to Import Orchids? If you plan to spirit into the United States foreign orchids you need to apply for a permit from the U.S. Department of Agriculture's Animal and Plant Health Inspection Service. For more information, see the **USDA Scientific Services** Web site (**http://www.aphis.usda.gov/ppq/ss**).

ORCHID LIST DIGEST PHOTO EXCHANGE
http://www.silverlink.net/~tcmeyers

This is where you can see photos of the orchids under discussion in the Orchid List Digest Archives.

ORCHIDS-CAN MAILING LIST

*A mailing list for Canadian orchid fans. To subscribe e-mail majordomo@chebucto.ns.ca with **subscribe orchids-can** in the body of the message.*

ORCHID BIOLOGY DISCUSSION LIST
http://www.bdt.org.br/listas/orchid-biology

Tap into this Web site for directions for joining the list and a link to messages and subscribers.

GARDENWEB ORCHID FORUM
http://www.gardenweb.com/forums/orchids

*Tap into GardenWeb (**http://www.gardenweb.com**) to have bulletin board-style discussion about orchid care, mail-order sources, and other orchid topics.*

THE USENET ORCHID NEWSGROUP

*To tap into the newsgroup **rec.gardens.orchids** you need to subscribe with your newsreader or browser. Head to Chapter 1 for instructions.*

Free Help from Web Sites of Orchid Societies

You'll find lots of orchid societies on the Web. Some offer only membership information on their Web sites, but others offer growing advice and pictures of members' orchids. You can find a list of orchid society Web sites at: Orchidlink's Society Page (**http://www.orchidlink.com/society.htm**). You should also take a look at WWW Sites for Orchid Societies and Organizations (**http://www.chebucto.ns.ca/Recreation/OrchidSNS/wsociety.html**).

Here are some of our favorite Web sites:

THE AMERICAN ORCHID SOCIETY
http://orchidweb.org

ORCHID SOCIETY OF CALIFORNIA
http://www.wundergrow.com/osc.html

AUSTRALIAN NATIVE ORCHID SOCIETY
http://www.ozemail.aust.com:80/~graemebr

ORCHIDMANIA OF SOUTH FLORIDA
http://www.orchidmania.org

ORCHID SOCIETY OF NOVA SCOTIA
http://www.chebucto.ns.ca/Recreation/OrchidSNS/orchid.html

OREGON ORCHID SOCIETY ONLINE
http://www.teleport.com/~gblastn

free Help Growing Palms & Cycads

Maybe we love palms because we they evoke memories of the Garden of Eden. Or perhaps it's because they remind us that we need a Hawaiian vacation. If you think your climate is too cold to grow palms, we have good news. (No, you don't need to saw skylights into your roof and jack up the thermostat.) There are Web sites that will show you how to grow palms in chilly climates like those of the East Coast.

And have you ever thought about growing cycads? Cycads are ancient seed plants topped by a crown of big leaves. Cycads hail from the Permian Age of the dinosaurs, 200 million years ago. You'll find cycads growing in southern Florida and Australia. Even if they're not the sort of thing to plant in your northern Michigan trailer camp, we guarantee that you'll still enjoy the Web sites about them. They offer marvelous pictures and insight into these amazing plants.

 PALM AND CYCAD SOCIETIES OF FLORIDA
http://www.plantapalm.com/index.htm
Tap into the Virtual Palm and Virtual Cycad Encyclopedias. Be sure to take a look at the delightful Virtual Palm Tour of Fairchild Tropical Garden. There's a mailing list for palm and cycad lovers, and links to other Web resources about these plants.

PALM INFORMATION
—PALM TREES, TROPICALS, SUBTROPICALS
http://www.homestead.com/donselman
What do bugs, palms, and thunderstorms have in common? Learn the answer to this and much more at this friendly, informative site from Dr. Henry Donselman, a palm specialist. (Okay, since you asked, according to Donselman, a macroburst thunderstorm is also known as a "palmetto pounder," since the fierce drops can supposedly crush palmettos, but it's unclear whether meteorologists are referring to palmetto plants or bugs.)

FAIRCHILD TROPICAL GARDEN
http://www.ftg.org/index.html

This is the Web site for the preeminent botanical garden in Miami. There's a searchable herbarium and garden plantings database, as well as a Florida flora gallery.

INTERNATIONAL PALM SOCIETY
http://www.palms.org

A PRACTICAL GUIDE TO GERMINATING PALM SEEDS
http://www.palms.org/principes/1999/palmseeds.htm
Reprinted from the April 1999 issue of Palms, the journal of the International Palm Society.

PALM AND CYCAD SOCIETY OF AUSTRALIA
http://www.pacsoa.org.au

 **THE CYCAD SOCIETY**
http://www.cycad.org
You'll find a newsletter, links to Web information about cycads, and a mailing list.

THE CYCADS PAGES
http://plantnet.rbgsyd.gov.au/PlantNet/cycad/index.html
Ken Hill runs this beautiful site for the Royal Botanic Gardens in Sydney, Australia.

THE VIRTUAL PALM ENCYCLOPEDIA
http://www.plantapalm.com/vpe/vpe_index.htm
The Palm & Cycad Societies of Florida offer the consummate online guide to all-things palm, including articles on the fossil records and economic impacts of palms. Even if you don't have a palm in your backyard, you'll find hours of fascinating reading. You'll even find the lyrics to Jimmy Buffet's song Lone Palm.

 ## Free Help for Growing Palms in Not-So Tropical Climates

THE COOL TROPICS
http://www.compassnet.com/hueppi/tropics/tropics.htm
This cool site details how you can set up a tropical paradise, complete with palms and cycads, in your own snow-covered backyard.

THE HARDIEST PALM
http://www.libertynet.org/bgmap/hardiplm.html
Mark Glicksman, who lives in a suburb of Philadelphia, explains why the needle palm, or Rhapidophyllum hystrix, is his candidate for hardiest palm on earth.

GROWING HARDY PALMS
http://surf.to/hardypalms
Leonard Holmes tells you which palms are the hardiest, what the USDA zone numbers mean in regard to palms, and where you can buy palms on the Internet.

HUW'S PLEASURE GARDEN
http://www.treetops.u-net.com/home.html

Huw Collingbourne explains how you can grow a subtropical paradise in the chilblain-inducing climates of Britain.

EXOTIC PLANTS IN A COOL CLIMATE
http://homepages.nildram.co.uk/~jimella/exotic.htm

Jim Jottings explains how ambitious gardeners can grow exotic plants in chilly gardens.

THE HARDIEST PALMS
http://ourworld.compuserve.com/homepages/tjwalters/

Tom Walters tells you how to turn your frosty yard into a tropical paradise. He offers palm winter protection advice, a guide to palm and seed sources, USDA zone maps, and hardy palm lists.

For more palm Web sites head to
Ed Ladd's Searching the Internet for Palms
(**http://mahpro.com/palmsch.html**).

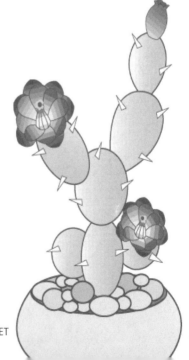

CHAPTER 25

free Help Growing Cacti

Those of us who live in USDA Zone 3 tend to think of cacti as those scouring pads in pots that double as houseplants for the watering can-challenged. But anyone who's traveled a desert knows that cacti can be as evocatively beautiful as a sunset, especially when blooming. Whether you need help watering the cactus mom and dad gave you for your dorm room, or you dream of cacti as big as architectural wonders towering over your backyard, there are Web sites that will help you.

🕲 ***Warning!*** *Gloria was once given a cactus as a gift. While driving home, the cactus tipped over and Gloria threw an arm around it like one would a child. She was picking needles out of her hand and arm for days. If you grow cacti, keep them far from kids and pets.*

 Big Web Sites for Cactus and Succulent Lovers

CACTUS AND SUCCULENT PLANT MALL
http://www.cactus-mall.com/index.html
This is a must-bookmark site. You'll find regular updates of plant care information, plus lists of suppliers.

THE SUCCULENT PLANT PAGE
http://www.graylab.ac.uk/usr/hodgkiss/succule.html
A wonderful resource with information on raising, growing, and caring for cacti and other succulents.

JUSTIN SPIEGEL'S DESERT CACTUS PAGE
http://www.desertcacti.com
Justin updates his site weekly with new cactus growing advice. Be sure to check the articles archive to read about fertilizer, endangered species, and artificial lighting.

CACTUS CLUBS BY COUNTRY
http://www.cactus-mall.com/clubs.html

Find out if there's a cactus club in your country, courtesy of the Cactus and Succulent Plant Mall.

THE GREAT CACTI AND SUCCULENT WEB SITE
http://wkweb5.cableinet.co.uk/bingodog/cac.htm

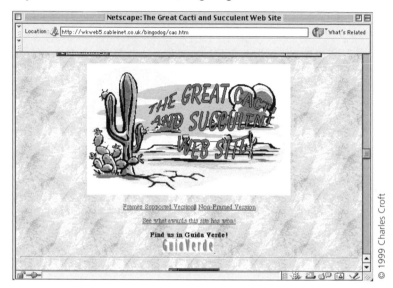

Charles Croft shares his extensive knowledge and his online library. There's a section on Kew Gardens, Britain's largest public cactus and succulent collection.

QUICK GUIDE TO CACTUS CARE
FROM CACTUS CREATIONS
http://myadnet.com/care2.html

"CARE OF THE CACTUS IN YOUR HOME"
BY DALE T. LINDGREN, THE UNIVERSITY OF
NEBRASKA EXTENSION
http://www.ianr.unl.edu/pubs/Horticulture/g187.htm

CHRISTMAS CACTUS INFORMATION
FROM FERNLEA FLOWERS LTD.
http://www.fernlea.com/xmas/cactinfo.htm

 *Cactus Discussion Groups*

THE CACTI_ETC MAILING LIST
http://www.hpl.hp.com/botany/public_html/cacti_etc/html/join
list.html
Or, email: listproc@opus.hpl.hp.com. In the message type:
subscribe cacti_etc yourname

CACTI_ETC ARCHIVE & PHOTOS
http://www.hpl.hp.com/bot/cactus_home
Help files, photos, and archives from the Cacti_etc e-mail
discussion list.

CACTI AND SUCCULENTS FORUM
AT THE GARDEN WEB
http://www.gardenweb.com/forums/cacti

CACTUS AND SUCCULENT MAILING LIST
http://www.cactus-mall.com/mlist/mlist.html

 Read More About the Desert in the Web E-zine
Desert USA Magazine
(**http://www.desertusa.com**). Articles include stories like
"The Haunted Desert," profiles of famous desert
denizens, and a plant and an animal of the month.

 Cactus Postcards
E-mail your pals free cactus postcards
from Aztechlinks
(**http://www.aztechlink.com/postcards/postcard.shtml**).

free Plant Glossaries, Dictionaries, & Directories

If you think "aerobic" is only a type of bouncing to thin one's thighs, you need to get yourself to a gardening glossary—fast! This chapter profiles gardening dictionaries and plant reference lists you can tap into on the Web. Did you know that the U.S. Department of Agriculture maintains a *huge* database of native plants, including names, symbols, and photos, which you can access on the Internet? Did you know that you can tap into a database of weeds at Rutgers University to identify those prickly plants that have been invading your squash patch? There are even Web sites that will show you how to pronounce plants' Latin names and tell you what they mean.

GREENWEB'S GARDENING GLOSSARY
http://www.boldweb.com/greenweb/glossary.htm
From "air layering" to "vermiculite," the Greenweb Glossary will fill you in on the meaning of critical gardening terms so that you never again need to feel like a bumpkin in the Wal-Mart gardening center.

GLOSSARY OF ROOTS OF BOTANICAL NAMES
http://garden-gate.prairienet.org/botrts.htm
If you're wondering what those Latin names mean, this is the site to check.

WEED IMAGES AND DESCRIPTIONS FROM RUTGER'S COOPERATIVE EXTENSION
http://www.rce.rutgers.edu/weeddocuments/index.htm

The PLANTS database offers identification information on plants in the United States and its territories.

THE PLANT NAMES PROJECT
http://pnp.huh.harvard.edu
The Royal Botanic Gardens, Kew; the Harvard University Herbaria; and the Australian National Herbarium together run the Plant Names Project (PNP). The hefty goal of this consortium is to create and maintain a comprehensive authority file for the names of all seed plants.

PLANTS TOXIC TO ANIMALS
http://www.library.uiuc.edu/vex/vetdocs/toxic.htm
Did you know that rhododendrons, oleander, and hyacinth are toxic to animals? Mitsuko Williams, a veterinary medicine librarian at the University of Illinois at Urbana-Champaign, provides a list of toxic plants, photos, conditions of poisoning, toxic principle, and clinical signs.

THE USDA PLANTS NATIONAL DATABASE
http://plants.usda.gov/plantproj/plants/index.html
Tap into PLANTS to identify native plants including wildflowers, shrubs, vines, trees, legumes, and grasses.

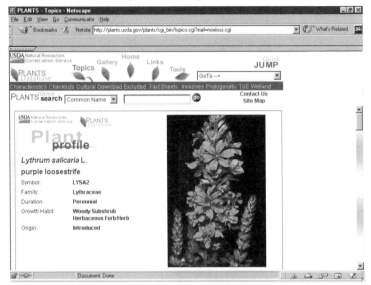

In the USDA's PLANTS database you can call up photos and information about noxious weeds by state.

THE CARNIVOROUS PLANT ARCHIVE
http://redtail.unm.edu/cp
Chris Frazier maintains a directory of Web sites that relate to carnivorous plants for those who would really rather be watching horror movies than watering chrysanthemums.

PLANT LINK
http://www.plantamerica.com/palink.htm
Over 88,000 plant names are included in this encyclopedia, which you can search by family, scientific name, or common name.

MEDICINAL AND POISONOUS PLANTS DATABASE
http://www.wam.umd.edu/~mct/Plants/index.html
Michael C. Tims of the University of Maryland, College Park maintains databases of both medicinal and poisonous botanicals.

TALKING PLANTS
http://www.talkingplants.com
"Our plant profiles," writes Ketzel Levine, "arranged in alphabetic order, offer the inside scoop on horticulture's Royal Families, as told by the one and only Doyenne of Dirt, part botanist, part biographer, and all slave."

GENUS OF THE WEEK
http://fisher.bio.umb.edu/pages/JFGenus/jfgenus.htm
This is a fun site for those who want to learn about plants. It's especially good for those who need to learn all those Latin names for their botany final.

BOTANY.COM, THE ENCYCLOPEDIA OF PLANTS
http://www.botany.com

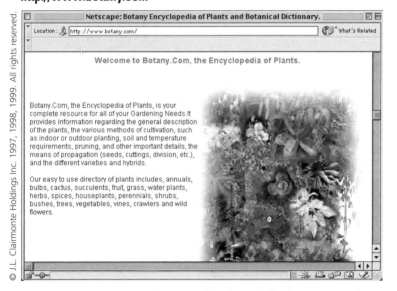

Bookmark this Web site. Its plant encyclopedia includes descriptions, cultivation information, soil and temperature requirements, information on pruning, and more. It also offers a guide to botanical gardens and societies, pests and diseases, and a dictionary of botanical names.

ABOUT THE AUTHORS

Judy Heim is an avid gardener who has been trolling the Internet for gardening advice for years. She's the author or co-author of 14 computer books, including *The Needlecrafter's Computer Companion.* She's written for *PC World* magazine for 15 years, and for 10 years authored a monthly Internet column for the magazine. She has written for *Family Circle, CNN Interactive, Newsweek, Cosmopolitan, PC/Computing, Family PC,* and many other magazines. Judy collects peonies.

Gloria Hansen is the co-author of eight Internet or computer-related books, including *The Quilter's Computer Companion.* In addition to enjoying gardening, Gloria is an award-winning quiltmaker. Her work, which is often designed using a Macintosh computer, has appeared in numerous magazines, books, and on television. She has written articles for leading computer magazines (including *Family Circle* and *PC World*) and craft publications

(including *Art/Quilt Magazine* and *McCalls's Quilting*), and she writes the "High-Tech Quilting" column for *The Professional Quilter.* You can visit her Web page at **http://www.gloriahansen.com.** Gloria lives in East Windsor Township, New Jersey.

BIBLIOGRAPHY

Heim, Judy and Gloria Hansen, *Free Stuff for Quilters,* C&T Publishing, Concord, CA,1998

._____. *Free Stuff for Crafty Kids* C&T Publishing, Concord, CA,1999

._____. *Free Stuff for Collectors* C&T Publishing, Concord, CA, 2000

._____. *Free Stuff for Sewing Fanatics,* C&T Publishing, Concord, CA,1999

._____. *Free Stuff for Stitchers,* C&T Publishing, Concord, CA,1999

._____. *The Quilters Computer Companion,* No Starch Press, San Francisco, CA, 1998

Heim, Judy, *The Needlecrafter's Companion,* No Starch Press, San Francisco, CA, 1999

INDEX

For more information on other fine books from C&T Publishing, write for a free catalog:

C&T Publishing, Inc., P.O. Box 1456, Lafayette, CA 94549

(800) 284-1114

http://www.ctpub.com   e-mail: ctinfo@ctpub.com

FREE STUFF ON THE INTERNET SERIES

Free Stuff for Crafty Kids
Includes Web sites that offer kid-friendly projects, such as origami, kites, sewing, rubber stamps, holiday crafts, cartooning, and more.

Free Stuff for Sewing Fanatics
Free stuff for all kinds of sewing topics, including sewing machine help, dollmaking, serging, and patterns, and bridal sewing.

Free Stuff for Stitchers
An up-to-date list of sites that offer the best free stuff for stitchers, knitters, and beaders! More advice than you could read in a lifetime.

Free Stuff for Quilters, 2nd Edition
Over 150 updated new links on quilt patterns, discussion groups, and organizations, plus quilt shops to visit, how-tos, and galleries of textiles and fiber arts.

Free Stuff for Collectors
Includes Web sites just for collectors, such as discussion groups, tips for cleaning and restoring collectibles, market news, and more.

 **C&T PUBLISHING**   **www.ctpub.com**